DIDN'T SEE IT COMING
MARC STOIBER

MW00979099

TO

BIG WAVE SURFER,

STAY CURIOUS!

M.

For my parents, who encouraged me to
take risks, saying they'd pay for a flight
home if it all went terribly wrong.

For my kids, who forced me to rethink
my job.

And for my wife Colleen, who encouraged
me – again and again – to get the damn
book written.

—

ISBN-13: 978-1-5053-8900-5
ISBN-10: 1505389003

SET IN CALIBRE AND TIEMPOS TEXT
DESIGNED BY RETHINK

THIS ISN'T A BOOK FOR MARKETERS.

IT'S A BOOK FOR THINKERS WHO HAPPEN TO BE IN MARKETING, AND PERHAPS WONDERING WHY.

TABLE OF CONTENTS

FOREWORD

I'm the kind of person who never reads forewords.

You're obviously the kind of person who does.

So let me do my best to fulfill what I suspect is the mission of a proper foreword: To confirm that you made a wise decision in buying this book, and that you will indeed benefit from reading its contents. As well as giving you a bit of a flavour of what's to come, and of the character of the author.

I first met Marc Stoiber in 1995 when he landed in Vancouver after stints at ad agencies in several exotic lands. He was very young and very energetic and very tall. Today he is still two of those things.

He was also very innocent and idealistic in many ways. Over a surprisingly short period of time we created some great work together, turning an agency that was best known for its three-martini lunch into Canada's Agency of the Year three years in a row. Marc was a key part of this transformation, which taught him his first big lesson in creating brands: Start with your own.

After four years of success in Vancouver, Marc was ready for the big leagues. So I talked him into running the creative department at our newest office, moving his young family to the Big Show in marketing in Canada: Toronto.

That's where the trouble began. As you'll read in the chapters ahead, Marc's idealism ran smack dab into the realities of marketing in the post-911 era: Useless products sold by overly analytical people using media models that were obviously on their last legs.

Over the course of the next few years Marc lost his innocence, but gained something far more valuable: Real insight into what is wrong with modern marketing and some interesting hunches on how to change things for the better.

They were more than hunches, really. In fact, they were the catalyst for the creation of a new kind of marketing agency, which Marc created against some very tough odds, during the height of the Great Recession.

Since our paths diverged in the early 2000s, Marc and I continued to collaborate on the odd project. And I started a company called Rethink, which sought to answer some of the very same questions Marc was so pointedly asking. Our journeys have been different, but our goal has been the same: To find a more human way to talk to people about products and services that can enrich their lives.

I think you'll find Marc's journey fascinating, and his conclusions thought-provoking— dare I say even useful. If you're like me, you'll steal some of his best ideas and pass them off as your own.

Some of these ideas are Marc's, learned the hard way, through trial and error. Others come from some very smart people he's met along the way. Still others come from interesting case studies Marc has sleuthed out from innovative companies around the world.

All of his conclusions share a few common traits: They're based on common sense. They're rooted in positive values. And they're dead simple. With not a hint of marketing jargon to be seen.

By the end of this book I think you'll feel entertained, enlightened and maybe even a little bit inspired.

You also just might feel a little better about the future of marketing and your own role within it. Yes, there are many things wrong with this business. But with the right attitude and a few simple principles, it is possible to be an Ad Man and feel good about how you're spending your life.

Over to you, Marc.

CHRIS STAPLES

Chris is a founding partner with Rethink,
with offices in Vancouver, Toronto and Montreal.

INTRO–DUCTION

STRANGE DAYS, INDEED

I'll never forget the day.

I was creative director at a multinational ad agency, and my team had been drafted to breathe new life into the comatose Mr. Clean account.

We were doing well. Mr. Clean was en route to becoming Procter & Gamble's global turnaround of the year. Go team.

This particular day, one of the account service people walked into my office clutching an array of Mr. Clean bottles filled with brightly colored liquids.

"Spring, summer, autumn, winter scents!" he declared. They were all new, created expressly to cajole North American homemakers into buying a bottle of Mr. Clean every season, even if there was still a half-full bottle in the cupboard. After all, you wouldn't want your floor smelling like spring if it was summer.

Really?

I looked at my account person. He looked at me. Someone in the last row of the imaginary audience coughed, and we called it a day.

That evening, I talked to my wife about the dim bulb of doubt that was glowing in my head. "Does the world really need four more flavors of floor cleaner?" I asked.

Her answer, a simple "No," pretty much ruined my life.

Because when you work in advertising and you finally realize the world doesn't need what you're selling, you're screwed. I was screwed.

As the bulb of doubt began to glow more brightly, I saw the insanity everywhere. Most of the products I marketed could've gone straight to landfill without consumers missing a beat. The millions spent on advertising this stuff, meanwhile, could've been redirected to charity or (drumroll please) innovating products that actually improved the human condition. Either way it would've bought the company more goodwill.

And that was just the stuff *I* was selling. When I took a hard look at *all* the products advertised around me, my mood got very dark indeed. How did I not see the pointlessness of all this before?

As you might imagine, my days in Big Agencyland were numbered. I quit my job and set out on a career journey that, over the course of ten years, would expose me to some tectonic shifts in marketing. The rise of sustainability. The explosion of social media. The exodus of bright minds from communication to innovation.

As it happens, my journey also coincided with upheaval on a much larger scale. Entire countries went bankrupt. Millions of North Americans lost their homes, their savings, their stake in the American Dream. Our pillars of prowess evaporated; the only things we seemed to still manufacture were inscrutable investment schemes. We went through the deepest recession since '29.

I'm no economist. I'm no captain of industry. But I do have a talent for connecting dots and making complicated things simple.

What I saw as I wandered through these strange days were new dots that hadn't been connected. Simple new ideas that were sprouting up where the dinosaurs had fallen.

Today I feel more excited about the state of my business than I have in a long time. Sure, everything has gone topsy-turvy. Inviolable institutions have crumbled (or need some serious reno). But everywhere, there are opportunities for the brave and open-minded. So what do we need to unlock them?

BREAK YOUR BELIEF FRAMEWORK

Belief frameworks are funny things.

As the name implies, they're structures that shelter us from confusion. They give order to our world, eliminate background noise, reassure us that things are as we believe they are. At the same time, they tend to slam the door shut on new perspectives that could help us grow.

As you might imagine, rigid belief frameworks don't hold up well in rapidly evolving environments. They become cement shoes.

I found it paramount to question and prune my beliefs on a regular basis as I progressed along my journey. If you're going to get the most from this book, you should probably sharpen your own pruning shears.

So what sort of belief frameworks did I overhaul? Here's an easy one I started with—see if it resonates.

In high school, the career counselor asked me what I imagined myself doing for a living. I said I didn't know, but I saw myself getting off an airplane in a good suit.

As silly as it must've sounded (and still sounds), that 1970s suburban white kid belief framework of what success comprised became my scorecard. And, sure enough, I made it happen. I found a job that got me the corner office, the huge staff, people buying me drinks and quoting me in the press, business-class flights out the wazoo.

Of course, none of that stuff really mattered, I laughed with benign indifference from my tastefully appointed creative director throne on high. Symbols didn't define me.

Until they were gone.

When I left the big agency, all the symbols disappeared. It was as if HR had boxed and filed them.

Suddenly, Daddy didn't have to fly to New York anymore. His corner office was in the basement, next to the LEGO set.

Oooooh, that hurt.

On the bright side, the rude awakening led to personal growth in a weird, roundabout way.

It started with phone calls from colleagues in Adland, asking how I'd done it. Invariably, the conversations would progress from the romance of turning my back on it all to actually listing the trappings I'd traded in. That's where the chats would get a bit spiky and uncomfortable. Something like this:

> "Wow, I wish I had the balls to do what you did. I feel I'm just dancing for the shiny dollar, selling crap. But there's no way I could give up my [insert expensive habit here]. I swear I'm going to make the jump, too. Real soon."

Slowly, I realized my symbols of success were the foundation of a very real belief framework I had shared with my colleagues. I'd been forced to give up the symbols and look at the belief framework as an outsider would. As I became more detached from it, I started to see new possibilities.

That's how one belief framework got turned on its head. Here are a few others I had to work through.

Belief in an Infinite Planet

Ever been in an earthquake? There's nothing to match the feeling when you discover the ground isn't as steadfast as you thought.

In a sense, we're having our belief in planet Earth shaken every day now, as we discover the environment simply can't swallow up our excess and stupidity like a benevolent parent. A pretty big revelation for anyone whose business involves selling pointless consumption.

Belief in Growth

This one's linked to belief in an infinite planet. But it's also deeply ingrained in our Western concept of business success. A successful brand is one that grows. A successful business and company, ditto.

My involvement in the business sustainability movement, however, enlightened me to the fundamental flaw in this thinking. Infinite growth has no natural template. Even the mightiest tree grows to its natural limits, then happily falls over and becomes mulch for the forest. No bruised egos. No fired CMOs.

So how did our belief in never-ending growth (often at great personal cost) become a fundamental goal? Question that, and you start to question a bunch of enshrined business principles. Down the rabbit hole you go.

Belief in the Western World

Growing up, I always assumed that Jesus was blond, Hollywood defined storytelling, and products innovated in the "developed" world (aka Europe and North America) were the only ones worth their salt.

Thanks to global supply chains, the rising economic power of emerging nations, the Internet, and a dozen other factors I won't bore you with, our status as center of the universe has been seriously called into question, if not thrown out the window. How does it feel to be not so terribly important?

Belief in My Career

My friend Lorne Craig, also a reformed Adland veteran, put it best when he said, "I've decided to be a human being now, not a human doing." Ad guys give great sound bites.

Lorne has a point. My belief system always included a definition of self through career. I truly thought building brands was a noble mission. In fact, I was quite capable of justifying personal compromises as sacrifices for my extremely important career. What an idiot.

Thankfully, that belief was seriously curtailed. I can tell you, however, that knocking "career" off the podium of important things left a pretty big void in my psyche.

Belief in My Ability to Make a Difference

This links directly to the belief in my career. Once I realized my creative director job wasn't going to make me a better human being, I had to step back and see how else I was making a difference in the world. Short, brutal answer: I wasn't.

Not one to dwell on past shortcomings, I vowed to immediately start adding value to humanity.

In my missionary zeal, I undertook the writing of this book. The results might not be on par with discovering penicillin, but if it steers a few marketers right, I'll sleep better.

I also sold my big house, and took my family on a six month surfing trip to Bali. If you don't see the connection between surfing and adding value to humanity, you've never surfed. I firmly believe a world with more surfers would mean a world with fewer warmongers, oil czars, and Wall Street hedge fund managers. We could all breathe a sigh of collective relief.

Belief in My Expertise

After loudly proclaiming my intent to write this book, I sat down at the keyboard and...nothing. All I could muster was a table of contents that would've produced an anemic facsimile of a B-grade business book. I simply wasn't an expert.

I sent out a distress signal to my friend John Marshall Roberts. John calls himself a "mad scientist," but he's truly an expert in belief frameworks and unlocking human potential.

He got straight to work on me, asking what I believed I was best at.

Connecting dots and simplifying things, I said. So, he reasoned, why not forget about coming up with one mind-bending expert thought and simply write down all the smart ideas I'd collected and connected? Oh, I replied. And make it funny and readable. Oh.

It worked. Turns out I'm an expert, after all.

Belief in Brands

As I've journeyed along, another dim bulb of doubt has started to glow more brightly. I still read ad journals and track leading brands. Something feels, well, different. The promises they're selling look increasingly tired and superficial, even cynical and disingenuous. It's a bit as if brands are religion, and the congregation has moved on to science.

Perhaps I'm just old, grumpy, and yearning for an irretrievable past. But maybe, just maybe, I'm connecting imperceptible dots that others aren't seeing. Are brands on their way out, about to be replaced by something more reflective of our rapidly evolving beliefs?

WHERE DID MY BRANDS GO?

And that, gentle reader, is the point of this book.

I believe brands as we know them are toast.

I've touched on the state of flux our world is in. This upheaval has shaken the belief frameworks of a great number of people. These folks simply aren't going to look at brands—a business construct from a bygone era—and love them without question. They know too much and have come too far. You can't put the toothpaste back in the tube, to use a tired cliché.

Does this mean brands are going to go away? And what will replace them?

I don't have the definitive answer to either question. I do, however, have incredible faith in the power of smart people.

This book is a challenge to all you smart folks out there. It lays a foundation I believe we can collectively build on.

My foundation may be imperfect. Heck, the Internet was an imperfect platform. But pretty cool things happened when forward-thinking people built on the Internet, probably in ways its founders never envisioned.

So let's get to work.

PART I.

THE WORLD I SEE:

IN WHICH WE EXPLORE A SOCIETY RAVAGED BY OVER-CONSUMPTION

MY CAREER IS OVER

YEARNING FOR *MAD MEN*

I started my advertising career in Hong Kong. It was 1989, the last hurrah of colonial excess before the Brits turned off the gin tap and handed the island wistfully back to the Chinese.

And there I was. Twenty-three years old, fresh off the plane and job hunting in my double-breasted blazer, chinos, and heavy black brogues, hair slicked back to artfully emphasize my huge ears and nose.

What I lacked in style, I made up for in chutzpah. I knew creative directors were notoriously hard to get in front of. So I simply showed up, told receptionists a story about being the CD's old friend, and barged right in. Sometimes it actually worked.

On one such occasion, I waltzed into the office of Grey's CD Chris Kyme, and I made it immediately clear he should hire me. Chris laughed out loud, said I looked like a young Prince Charles, and gently shooed away the agitated receptionist who'd tailed me down the hall. He then asked if I liked Sleng Teng reggae and popped a tape into his blaster.

Head bobbing to the Sleng Teng, Chris looked at my portfolio of work. The ads I'd done were pathetic, but I was in the right place at the right time. He needed a warm body who could string English sentences together. I got the job.

Over the course of three years, Chris helped me become a decent "creative." He taught me how to craft solid copy, create strong ad concepts, and love ad culture.

Let me expand on that last point.

At the time, advertising wasn't just a career. It was a culture unto itself, complete with tribes, high priests, and insane ceremonies of the faith called award shows.

Chris hailed from London, the Vatican of ad culture in the 1970s and 1980s. He'd come from a "hot shop" agency and had hung out with people at other hot shops. They dressed outrageously, shot commercials in Tahiti, drank too much, did drugs, threw food around the best restaurants, and generally lived like rock stars.

What's not to love?

Unfortunately, despite the efforts of folks like Chris, Hong Kong was an outpost of ad culture. We did ads quick and cheap. We couldn't find outrageous clothing in our size (I'm a very non-Asian six foot three inches). And while there was community among creatives, we couldn't hold a candle to London in its glory.

In my heart of hearts, however, I knew one day I'd rise to take my rightful place among the ad culture illuminati.

It never quite happened. Perhaps I wasn't good enough. Perhaps my choices—shops I worked at, art directors I partnered with, clients I served—didn't click. Or perhaps my timing was simply wrong.

The more I think about it, the more I put it down to timing. Here's why.

When I started in advertising, computers didn't exist. Ditto the Internet. In fact, the way we created ads, the media we placed ads in, and the structure of ad agencies (not to mention agency fees) hadn't really changed since the 1950s.

Among other things, this lack of upheaval allowed the ad world to create its own culture at a thoughtful, leisurely pace. What it became, especially from the 1960s to the 1980s, was the Hollywood of commerce.

Unlike Hollywood, however, advertising didn't create entertainment for the sake of entertainment. It did so to sell the client's product. So when the technological upheaval of the 1990s happened, ad agencies didn't just have to rip apart their storytelling structures, as Hollywood did. They also had to deal with a rash of new, powerful clients from the tech world. Clients with their own culture of cool, who didn't understand why they should show deference to a bunch of old ad dudes in black turtlenecks.

Like many in advertising, I welcomed the change. Sure, I never experienced the New York and London heyday. But a new world order was being defined. Venerable old brands were being upended by dot-coms. Old agency thinking was being torched. Vive la revolution, and all that.

Besides, I could always watch *Mad Men* if I felt like seeing old friends.

BILL BERNBACH IS DEAD

As the upheaval gathered steam, I was busy gathering work experience. Following my stint at Grey Hong Kong, I worked at BBDO Germany, then joined an upstart agency in Vancouver named Palmer Jarvis. Once again, it was right place, right time. I got to work under ad-Yoda Ron Woodall and his brilliant young protégé, Chris Staples. I joined the agency just in time to see it rocket to success, becoming our country's most-awarded shop for several years running.

This was particularly fun (in an admittedly juvenile way) because Vancouver was an ad backwater at the time, perennially in the shadow of Toronto. We loved beating the pants off Toronto agencies.

We were the pirates; they were the navy.

Then came the buyout.

When a hot shop becomes successful, it inevitably gets bought by a bigger agency or network of agencies. This makes sense on many fronts. The owner of the hot shop gets to relax and finally enjoy the fruit of his labor. The buyer gets an injection of revenue, vigor, and cool.

But for the employees of the hot shop, it feels a bit as if an ancient vampire is rejuvenating itself on your blood. Creepy.

We happened to be bought by Doyle Dane Bernbach, or DDB. In its 1960s heyday, it was the hottest of hot shops in New York. And Bill Bernbach reigned as the high priest of ad culture.

Bernbach was an incredible creative. His teams redefined advertising with work like the self-deprecating VW campaign. He changed the way ads were created, partnering writers and art directors for the first time. He was also a very quotable guy, a fountain of cool sound bites on the ad business. If he'd looked like George Clooney, he could've ruled the world. As it was, he completely dominated advertising in his day.

So if you're going to be bought, you could do worse than Bernbach's agency. Mind you, Bernbach had been dead fifteen years when we were acquired, but surely there was a bit of Bill's pirate spirit still left at head office. We were cautiously optimistic.

First signs were not auspicious. We were partnered with DDB Toronto, an agency that just couldn't exorcise its inner navy. They needed pirates. I volunteered.

The first thing I did when I arrived as DDB Toronto's new creative director was stroll the halls. At every door, there was a small card with a Bernbach quote, reminding us how clever the old man was. Hmm.

Then, in the reception area, I saw it. A large oil painting of Bill Bernbach, looking like a university dean. Gilt frame, the works. My jaw dropped.

I jumped on the phone with Chris Staples, my boss and confidante in Vancouver.

"Chris, they've got an oil painting of Bill in the reception."

"You gotta be kidding."

"I know. What do I do?"

"Marc, you've got to get rid of Bill."

The following weekend, I snuck back into the agency, took Bill off the wall, and replaced him with a tasteful painting of five dogs playing poker. Personally, I think Bill would've approved.

Monday morning, all hell broke loose. New York had been notified and was incensed. Frank Palmer, head of Palmer Jarvis—notoriously fond of pranks himself and not one to let anyone rattle his cage—called me nervously from Vancouver.

"Marc, where's Bill?"

"He's dead, Frank."

"You didn't destroy the painting, though? New York's pissed."

"Of course I didn't. Do I need to put Bill back?"

Frank paused. He let out a quiet chuckle. "No."

With that laugh, we tore down a tiny piece of the powerful brand erected by old-school ad culture. We didn't rip apart any infrastructure or blow up the hierarchies. But it was, to paraphrase Otter in *Animal House*, a situation that absolutely required a really futile and stupid gesture. And we were just the guys to do it.

"NEW!" ISN'T NEW

My industry, any industry, any person in any industry, heck, *everybody* needs a regular infusion of new thinking to thrive. Advertising, however, has a surprisingly uncomfortable relationship with new.

Why is this?

In a nutshell, new thinking scares big clients. It scares them because it may scare their consumers, and that may drive those consumers to the competition.

To avoid freaked-out consumers, big clients planning a communications campaign go through exhaustive research to gauge consumer reactions to insights, copy, layout, finished ads, everything.

Three things come out of research.

First, you get ads with all the interesting, pointy bits sanded off. If you're testing for approval with the largest possible number of people, you're going to have to delete things that could offend anyone. That's a lot of cutting. What you're left with is about as exciting as, well, 90 percent of the boring ads you ignore on your screen.

Second, research generates a stack of information the CMO can cover his or her butt with in case the campaign tanks. And, yes, they do tank on a regular basis. Remember, you're ignoring that 90 percent of boring ads on your screen.

And the final thing that comes from big research? A big paycheck for research companies. Go figure.

This culture of caution makes big advertising feel out of touch and irrelevant. Natalie Zmuda of *Advertising Age* described it best in her story "Ad Campaigns Are Finally Reflecting Diversity of US" (http://adage.com/article/news/ad-campaigns-finally-reflects-diversity-u-s/292023/).

Zmuda profiles a raft of new commercials by big brands like GM and Coke that aired during the Sochi Olympics and Super Bowl. These spots showed mixed-race families, same-sex couples, people in wheelchairs, and even, yes, Muslims.

Zmuda's point is that while these images of diversity might be perfectly "so what?" for consumers, on Madison Avenue they're trumpeted as a great leap forward, an "All New!" in a flashing starburst. As Zmuda writes, "Marketing experts say this is the moment that historians and social commentators will likely declare a tipping point for advertising enlightenment in the years to come. But, in truth, adland is late to the game, and plenty of progress is still to be made."

Unfortunately, despite the upheaval threatening the ad business, big agencies and their big clients aren't going to stop the vanilla messaging madness. If anything, the more the palace gates are stormed by new ideas, the more big brands will draw the velvet curtains and retreat to the salon of low-risk thinking.

Of course, there's a bright side. For every dinosaur, there are dozens of mammals scurrying underfoot. Upstart companies that don't have the budget to research their communication into oblivion. Companies that have little to lose and everything to gain. Companies that are letting their fans do the communicating for them, instead of entrusting the message to big agency bureaucracy. Companies that don't care if they alienate a few folks, as long as the consumers they want are crazy happy.

Big brands may be dabbling with diversity now. Benetton was splashing it on billboards around the world with its United Colors of Benetton campaign...in 1986.

SHINY AWARDS, CORNER OFFICES

Working at big agencies for years, I saw countless campaigns suffer death by irrelevance. We took great ideas, then researched and second-guessed them into an early grave. It was a demoralizing, soul-destroying experience.

And yet we stayed. Why?

I think it came down to three things. We got paid lots, we did fake ads, and we won awards.

People who created ads made a ton of money back when agencies were fueled by large commissions on media buys. It wasn't unusual in the 1990s to see a thirty-year-old creative director earning a quarter-million dollars a year, all while showing up for work at ten in the morning dressed in a smelly Sex Pistols shirt, throwing his feet up on the designer desk, and doodling ideas with a Sharpie felt pen.

Sure, thirty-year-old stockbrokers made more. But they had to wear suits and pretend they were Republicans. The horror.

So what happened when our thirty-year-old hotshot CD got a brief from a big client that entailed a timid commercial with five rounds of research? He held his nose, tried to look on the bright side (*We'll shoot it with a hot director!*), then eased the pain by doing fake ads for his local deli/liquor store/gym. These "fakies" were edgy, free for the client, and if they ran once in a public medium—late-night TV, photocopied poster hanging in the client's office—they were, in the spirit of Clinton and Lewinsky, technically no longer fake.

The fakies were then entered in awards shows, at great cost to the agency. They won awards, despite the judges grumbling that the ads probably weren't legit. Having won awards, they were hung up in the agency to prove the CD knew how to do edgy work. Big clients, despite hating the fact *they* didn't get award-winning work like that from the CD, surreptitiously basked in the "edgy agency" aura, bankrolling the whole venture with more timid commercial projects. Meanwhile, the CD bemoaned the big client's lack of vision and looked for the next fakie opportunity to ease the pain of artistic compromise.

As you might imagine, this system led to no small amount of cynicism and burnout. Although the money and awards were great, many of us started to wonder if that's all there was.

David Baker, a friend of mine who helps ad agencies and design firms escape this cycle of compromise, had an interesting observation. "People wonder why there are few fifty-year-old ad creatives but many fifty-year-old lawyers. It's because lawyers go into the game knowing they want to make tons of money—period. They do just that, and they're happy. Ad creatives, on the other hand, go into the game knowing they want to make beautiful ads. Inevitably, the system hammers this ideal to a pulp, leaving the creative with a big salary, expensive habits, and the dejection of having sold out. So they leave at fifty and become artists or coffee shop owners, bitter that it took them so many years to see through the system."

NEW TACTICS AREN'T CHANGE

Not so long ago, social media was lauded as a game changer. It would forever alter the relationship between brands and consumers.

Not so much.

Social media is a tactic. The way websites, ambient media, guerilla media, and product placements (that is, writing Pottery Barn into a *Friends* script) are tactics.

When they were new, each of these tactics was hailed as game changers. Why? I believe it's because communications folk have an insatiable hunger for incremental innovation. That is, stuff-that's-new-but-not-so-new-it-might-upset-the-applecart innovation.

Don't get me wrong. I love the way social media lets you conduct DIY research, asking consumers what they want from your company. If nothing else, it loosens the choke hold research companies have put on agencies for so long.

I also love that you can turn your fans into your media channel via social media, empowering them to tell all their friends about your company. I don't see TV, print, or billboard ads going away anytime soon, but isn't it nice to play the social card when you're negotiating with TV or newspaper media reps? You'll get a better deal, and perhaps even a few freebie basketball tickets to make nice.

My point is, the fundamental bit hasn't really changed at all. Client goes to agency with product and tells agency what she wants to say about it. Agency takes money and does communicating using all the creativity and tools at its disposal. Insert latest tactic here.

However, very few (if any) agency people ask the client if the world needs this product, if this product will improve the human condition, if there is any real *burning belief* in the product. That would be the sort of communications innovation that would give clients pause and give agency bean counters heart palpitations.

That, my friend, would be a game changer.

Arrogant bastard, you're saying. What gives you the right to decide what is and isn't a worthy product?

Nothing. I'm just one voice. But if my experience connecting dots is anything to go by, big changes often start with uncomfortable thoughts.

So here's a thought to start us off: products that hurt or kill people shouldn't be advertised.

I hear the howls of derision rising. Does that include fast food and pharma? Don't consumers need to take personal responsibility? What if a product helps some but hurts others? What if a company makes good and not-so-good products? How will all the makers of "bad" products survive?

Beats me.

But what if we could put together a few thousand bright minds and pose that question to them? Then try out a few of their solutions, learn from the experience, and repeat the exercise again and again?

We may never see products that hurt people banned from advertising. But pushing ourselves to think—and pursue—uncomfortable thoughts would certainly keep the business fresh.

Companies like IBM are already doing just that with their Global Idea Jams. If you aren't familiar with the concept, IBM invites thousands of smart people from around the world to "jam" on an idea over the course of forty-eight hours. They link together—demonstrating IBM's power to connect—and come up with, blend, and build on ideas. Cool thing is, you can sign in over your morning coffee, see an idea that was shaped the night before in a different part of the world, add your two cents, then send the idea off to be bashed about by other folks. Good fun.

When the exercise wraps, IBM has reams of controversial, uncomfortable new ideas, and all of us feel warm and fuzzy about participating.

Sure, it's just a tactic to get bright, off-the-wall thoughts into the company coffers. But it also sows the seeds for real change.

DRAFTED INTO *LA RÉSISTANCE*

To this point I've posited a raft of gripes about the business I love. Now for the good news.

If you see a problem, and you actively dig into it, a solution will inevitably appear.

For about a year, I grew increasingly frustrated with the lack of real change in advertising. Then I discovered sustainability.

You laugh.

Seriously, back in 2005 sustainability simply wasn't on the radar. Big brands didn't talk about it. And if big brands didn't want it, big agencies certainly weren't going to waste resources pushing it.

I had relocated from Toronto to Vancouver with my big agency. As inevitably happens on the left coast, I met people who were building companies based on new ideas. In this case, sustainable products. I was intrigued.

No, I didn't discover my inner environmentalist. I didn't look for a tree to chain myself to. But I found that products innovated with "green" as one of their criteria simply looked and felt different.

And while many of them didn't work as well as their mainstream counterparts did, I found their creators' passion for big innovation refreshing. These were people who wanted to change the world, not create floor cleaner with seasonal scents. If version 1.0 didn't nail it, they threw themselves completely into version 2.0.

For the first time in years, I felt excited about my career again. As a person used to marketing products that were indistinguishable from one another, I snapped to attention at the prospect of selling stuff with a whole new twist. These products *were* new. They didn't just have *New!* in a starburst on the packaging.

One obstacle remained. As a successful marketer, I was a driver of *unsustainability*. How would I ever gain the trust of potential clients who were passionate about rethinking the system I had helped create? In simple English, wouldn't they just tell me to go to hell?

They didn't. As I was germinating how to make the leap, I met with several key leaders of the business sustainability movement in Vancouver—folks like Joel Solomon, Peter Ter Weeme, and Robert Safrata. They were genuinely excited at the prospect of me marketing green products. It was as if they'd been waiting for someone from the dark side to join them.

As they introduced me to more people in the movement, I began to feel like a lone saboteur who had befriended someone in the French Resistance. Suddenly, I saw a vast network of collaborators, each with a burning desire to create a better world. It was as if I were back on Frank Palmer's pirate ship taking on the big agency navy.

I jumped in and started a green ad agency named Change. I had a terrific logo. I had a cool office. I didn't have a clue how to run a company. When you spend your career ensconced in a big agency creative department, you become a specialist, not an all-rounder. I had to learn how to pitch, budget, bill, and schedule my accounts. Not to mention paying the rent and my employees, and emptying the garbage.

For five years, we rode the roller coaster. Winning accolades for our great work, chewing shoe leather when the money ran out, and everything in between. At the end of it all, I sold the company to an excellent innovation firm and walked out with my head held high.

I also walked out with some great learning on sustainability in business:

- When I started Change, everyone congratulated me by saying, "Wow, you are so cutting-edge." I later discovered that when you're paying the bills, cutting-edge is a lousy place to be. Cutting-edge is fine if you're working for NASA with a steady paycheck. Today, people congratulate me on my consulting work by saying, "Wow, you are so right place, right time." Much better place to be.
- Small clients are great when you're in a big agency and frustrated with the timidity of your big clients. They're the source of bound-

less fakie ads. In a small agency, though, edgy small clients aren't great. They can't pay the bills.

- Big clients, much to my surprise, didn't want to talk about sustainability in their ads. They recognized that putting *Now More Sustainable!* on the label or commercial was shorthand for *Doesn't work as well and costs more!* Mainstream consumers were still wary of green for reasons I'll dig into later. And big clients need mainstream consumers.

- Big clients did, however, want to build sustainability into their products for reasons that included efficiency, long-term supply chain security, and stakeholder support. In short, they wanted me to help them design products that were more sustainable. And then not talk about it.

Let me expand on that last point. When I discovered big clients wanted me to help them innovate green into their products, I quickly realized I needed innovation experts around me, not marketers. I went looking for potential buyers and discovered Maddock Douglas in Chicago. They bought my brain and my office furniture and made me their VP of green innovation. Unfortunately, this happened just as the Great Recession was ramping up, and the economy forced us to part ways after a great year.

That's the way it goes with *La Résistance*. You win battles; you lose battles. But if you're pushing for meaningful change, the war inevitably goes your way.

MY INESCAPABLE VOID

I've worked in advertising, design, sustainability, and innovation. Today, I'm a consultant who helps clients build the sort of future-proof brands I describe in the second part of this book.

I've also been on a terrific journey, often finding myself in unexplored territory.

I've broken down belief frameworks that held me back and have become more courageous about chasing dreams that other people find too risky to pursue.

So am I fulfilled? Hell no.

My head still plays games with me, convincing me my choices were a disaster. Every day I yearn for the simpler past I left behind.

What I've become better at, however, is enjoying the roller coaster and understanding we're all just making this up as we go along.

Jerry Seinfeld said, "Life is truly a ride. We're all strapped in and no one can stop it. When the doctor slaps your behind, he's ripping your ticket and away you go. As you make each passage from youth to adulthood to maturity, sometimes you put your arms up and scream; sometimes you just hang on to that bar in front of you. But the ride is the thing. I think the most you can hope for at the end of life is that your hair's messed, you're out of breath, and you didn't throw up." (http://www.goodreads.com/quotes/33313-life-is-truly-a-ride-we-re-all-strapped-in-and)

So now let's move on to the ride we've strapped ourselves into, shall we?

THE PARA–NOIA ERA

YELLOW ALERT!

After 9/11, the Department of Homeland Security introduced a color-coded threat level system that was supposed to tell us how likely a terrorist attack might be.

It didn't work.

As security technologist Bruce Schneier wrote on the eve of the system being dismantled, "The problem is that the color-coded threat levels were vague and long-term, and didn't correspond to useful actions people can take" (http://edition.cnn.com/2011/OPINION/01/28/schneier.terror.threat.level/). It seemed all the alerts did was make us feel jittery and paranoid. Worse yet, we didn't know exactly how jittery to be. Should I be more fearful when it's code orange or code yellow?

Happily, the system did benefit one group of citizens. Comedians found loads of jokes in its flaws, inconsistencies, and ham-fisted attempts at keeping the populace quiet and obedient. For example, David Cross pointed out there was a not-entirely-coincidental correlation between Bush government missteps and spiking terror alert levels. "It's a coincidence that the terror alert happened to go up after that French report saying that Bush knew about 9/11...and two days after they said there was absolutely no link between Saddam Hussein and Osama...and within thirty-six hours of mad cow disease and saying the government might be implicit in it...and literally the day after the report that Halliburton overcharged by $65 million...and after Bush's ratings plummeted...it's called coincidence, you hippie freak! These guys out there on their computers compiling cold, hard irrefutable facts—!*&% you! I'll see you at Burning Man, you freak!" (from his album *It's Not Funny*).

Comedy aside, I believe our cynical reaction to the terror alert system hints at a more pervasive phenomenon. We're growing mistrustful of traditional institutions and finding new ones to identify with.

Just take a look at what's happening with Millennials, the demographic just out of college and entering the workforce.

According to a recent Pew research study, record numbers of Millennials (as compared with Xer's and boomers) describe themselves as politically independent, religiously unaffiliated, and mistrustful of their fellow citizen. (http://www.pewsocialtrends.org/2014/03/07/millennials-in-adulthood/)

That isn't to say the Millennials have built a shack in the woods and tuned out. They've just found new people to listen to and follow. Each other.

At the 2014 SXSW conference, a media study presented by Crowdtap confirmed that Millennials find user-generated content 50 percent more trustworthy and 35 percent more memorable than other forms of content. (http://www.inc.com/abigail-tracy/millennials-trust-user-generated-content-above-all-else.html)

So, ordinary Joes and Janes filming themselves describing a major event are more trustworthy than a major network news anchor and team of reporters describing that event?

Seems hard to believe. Or does it? When I dial up network news these days, it seems I'm inundated by ratings-grabbing stories repeated over and over again. At least with YouTube, I can dial in a keyword and pick from hundreds of citizen journalist perspectives.

Ditto for entertainment. Ditto for endorsements and advertising.

It doesn't take much squinting to see that big change is afoot.

In this chapter, I want to explore some of the major drivers of this change—I call them the forces of chaos. Good Marvel Comics name.

I also want to describe the impact these forces of chaos are having on us. Understand this, and we have a glimmer into the psyche of the new consumer. The person we're trying to reach.

ECONOMIC UPHEAVAL

I'm not an economist. I'm not even particularly good at math. But I had no trouble understanding the dread and anxiety that hit people like a slo-mo heart attack when the economic bottom fell out in 2008.

I understood it because, in a way, my profession was responsible for it.

Let me backtrack sixty years to describe, from a marketer's perspective, how it all happened.

At the end of World War II, the US government and industrialists realized they needed to do something with all the factories that had churned out war supplies—pronto. If they didn't, they'd have massive unemployment and stagnation on their hands right when the country needed economic regeneration most.

What they created were consumer products. Lots of consumer products.

Of course, people accustomed to saving each piece of string weren't immediately going to jump out and consume themselves silly. They needed a little encouragement. Cue the marketing guys.

One of the first blockbuster marketing campaigns to come from this era was the *American Dream*. The phrase was coined by James

Truslow Adams in 1931 (http://www.loc.gov/teachers/classroommaterials/lessons/american-dream/students/thedream.html). While most people think of it as the rallying cry of postwar American optimism, it in fact entered popular thinking only when the folks at Fannie Mae used it to sell mortgages.

The slogan worked. Americans bought into the suburbs en masse. And once they'd moved into all those white-picket-fence suburban homes, they filled them with shiny new stuff. Cars with lots of chrome. TVs. Heaps of clothes for the closets. All the trappings of the American Dream.

In a stroke of genius, the marketing guys built a thing called planned obsolescence into the Dream. After all, if our happy suburbanite bought a car and kept it twenty years, the car factory could turn off the lights. So cars were built to look outdated after a couple of years. Black-and-white TVs were replaced by color TVs, then larger-screen TVs. Hemlines went up and down every season. Buy it today, chuck it tomorrow became the order of the day. And, quickly, the American Dream turned into the frantic state of keeping up with the Joneses.

After the war, the workforce shifted dramatically. Women, accustomed to keeping production running stateside while their men fought the Nazis, weren't keen on giving up their jobs when the boys came home. As a result, two-income families fueled the American Dream well into the 1960s. In the 1970s, inflation kept peoples' incomes rising, so they could keep up the purchasing. In the 1980s, a stock market boom did the same. The 1990s saw communism fall and Eastern Europeans line up to buy into their own version of the American Dream—which of course brought more prosperity to the US companies that sold the American Dream kit—everything from blue jeans to movies.

In the 1990s, we started to see the cracks in the now massive, bloated, hyperconsuming Dream. We pinned our cash flow hopes on the Internet, which promised prosperity by the click. That turned out to be a bubble, which ended as all bubbles do. We loaded up on credit cards we couldn't pay off. We kept moving into bigger houses with mortgages we couldn't afford—then used our mortgages to pay our credit bills. And, like a drumbeat, marketers whispered, "Consume, consume, consume" in our ears.

Remember George W. Bush telling us to do our part after 9/11...by shopping? That should've hit us like a slap with a sack of hammers, but it didn't. Consumption had become our religion. It could cure all ills. Lonely? Buy a friend. Fat? Buy a new body. Depressed? Buy more pills.

Then 2008 happened. The sociopaths on Wall Street had taken the pursuit of money to its insanely logical conclusion. The world as we knew it broke. Everything crashed.

This time, however, there was nothing on the horizon to save us. No more newbie consumers in Eastern Europe or Asia to sucker into the Dream. No more technological booms. No more debt to push to the ceiling. The Dream party was over, and the hangover hurt.

The trauma we've just been through can't be fixed with an app. The middle class in America has been gutted. A handful of oligarchs are buying the government and making average citizens very, very cynical about democracy. Asia is rising and shifting balances of power. Corporations have replaced their full-time staff with part-timers and outsourced production. Job security is out the window. Mistrust of vapid slogans is high, and the hyperconsumption caused by things like planned obsolescence is being recognized by more and more people as a nasty ploy to make shareholders rich at the expense of our planet.

Go ahead. Tell these people to buy themselves happy. I dare you.

THE PLANET IS FINE, BUT WE'RE NOT

Economic meltdown isn't the only problem making consumers catatonic. Not by a long shot.

Linear production on a finite planet. Now *that's* a problem.

Um, wait. Most consumers don't even understand what linear production on a finite planet *means*. So let me back up a bit.

I've never found a better, more entertaining introduction to the concept than *The Story of Stuff* (http://www.youtube.com/watch?v= 9GorqroigqM). In twenty minutes, host Annie Leonard takes us on an animated journey through modern consumer product creation and consumption: finding natural resources, turning them into goods, selling the goods, using them, and throwing them away.

This, as Leonard explains, is linear production, and it works just dandy if you have a planet with endless resources, endless capacity to absorb the pollution that comes with production and usage, and endless landfills to hold discarded goods.

It doesn't, however, work on a planet with finite resources and finite capacity to absorb the pollution and garbage we throw away. Our planet, for example.

Truth is, we're depleting our natural resources at an alarming rate (if you want the depressing stats, Leonard provides enough to give you night sweats). We're also poisoning ourselves with the pollution that comes from making and using consumer products, and we're running out of space to dump the stuff we no longer want. Let's not even get started with the social and economic messes we've created in an effort to keep prices low and purchase rates high.

Essentially, we're consuming ourselves to the brink of extinction.

A few years ago, this problem wasn't on the average North American's radar. We did our nasty production work overseas and buried our garbage out of sight. No fuss, no muss.

Then those annoying environmental activists came along, armed with cameras, the Internet, and facts. Suddenly we saw the by-products of our consumption up close and personal. Entire regions laid to waste. Rampant poisoning of populations. Endemic corruption fostered to keep cheap production lines humming. Countries on the verge of environmental collapse.

Our reaction? Most of us simply logged off or changed the channel and bought something nice to cheer ourselves up.

Corporations did their best to ease our worries. They swept the issue under the carpet with a tidal wave of disinformation, employing many of the same lobbyists and PR firms that helped big tobacco fight health regulation for years.

At this point, I want to introduce James Hoggan. Jim is a public relations professional and an authority on the connection between PR and climate change denial. He's also one of the most balanced, down-to-earth people I know, 180 degrees from tree hugger.

Jim witnessed up close and personal how agents of his profession were co-opted by big fossil fuel energy concerns to seed doubt in science and demonize the folks with the facts. His book *Climate Cover-Up* (http://www.desmogblog.com/climate-cover-up) is a page-turner that maps out case after case of successful climate change smoke-screening.

I asked Jim which campaigns took the cake for brazen bafflegab. Without hesitation he pointed to Clean Coal and Ethical Oil. Even the names sound like gold award winners in the spin category.

I won't unravel each case individually—you can check Jim's book for that—but in both instances, the game plan was the same. Companies sensing growing consumer concern surrounding the environmental impacts of their products (US coal and Canadian oilsands oil) funneled massive funds into a three-pronged attack that included:

- First, the creation of "Astroturf" (fake grassroots) organizations. These orgs mimicked authentic citizen groups in both their folksiness and tactics for influencing political action. Their agenda—to stop impending government regulation—just happened to coincide with the goals of their very non-grassroots corporate backers.
- Second, the creation of alternative experts to go toe-to-toe with

climate scientists. This played on the press's need for balanced journalism. If a climate scientist, backed by the research of thousands of other climate scientists, presented his point of view in a news story, it was de rigueur for the story's author to balance that point of view with a dissenting opinion. That way, readers could weigh the opinions and make up their own minds. More often than not, the "experts" presenting the view that contradicted climate science had few, if any, credentials to support their opinion. They were, however, adept at providing captivating sound bites that infused doubt into the climate science argument. As Hoggan said, "The problem is, scientists think people should listen to them simply because they're telling the truth. They're completely outgunned by pseudoexperts with great PR training and charming personalities. It's like putting altar boys up against the Mafia."

- Finally, the creation of a campaign to position the supporters of climate change regulation as radicals, zealots, and enemies of progress. In the case of clean coal, climate scientists and regulators were painted as lefties who wanted to destroy the US economy. In the case of oilsands oil, the opposition was positioned as friends of terrorists. Yes, terrorists.

Now the good news. Earth didn't play ball with the corporations. Our climate is changing at an accelerating pace. As grim as this sounds, it's positive news on two fronts.

First, the climate denier argument, despite being well funded and professionally executed, is looking more and more like damaged goods. So now we can move past the confusion and start thinking about action.

Second, it's good news because North American consumers have no patience and little memory. It's sad, but consumers won't pay attention if climate change progresses like a slow-motion car wreck. Well, the car wreck is happening in real time now. And it's happening in our backyard, not Bangladesh. We're paying attention all right.

In fact, climate change makes the news every day. Hurricanes in the southern states are getting deadlier. Droughts in the Midwest and California are becoming so extreme, entire towns are drying up and shutting down. Cities like Paris are banning cars because the air isn't breathable. The weather across North America and Europe is getting more intense and less predictable.

But this all brings us to another problem. As consumers move past denial and confusion, they aren't jumping to action. Instead, they're feeling depressed and resigned. They believe climate change is real, we've caused it, and it's beyond the point of no return. Best to just lie down and take the whipping.

The root of the problem is that our sense of self is tied to the products we currently consume. And nobody's painted a picture that marries product innovation with climate rescue. Consumers simply don't see enough cool, environmentally conscious stuff out there to buy—even though, in many cases, the stuff exists. The only choice, for many consumers, is no choice.

A little story to illustrate my point: Calgary, Alberta, the city I was born and raised in, was devastated in the summer of 2013 when the Bow River flooded. Homes—many in the wealthy part of town—were destroyed. Thousands of people were evacuated and relocated to shelters. The downtown towers that house executives who make their money turning the oilsands into Canada's greatest environmental blight were flooded. The Stampede, dubbed the "Greatest Outdoor Show on Earth" and icon of Calgary's Western can-do spirit, almost didn't happen.

In a *Financial Post* story, it was estimated Alberta would take a 5 percent annualized hit to its GDP in the quarter following the flood. There was CAD $5 billion lost in sectors from transport to food production (http://business.financialpost.com/2013/06/26/albertas-worst-flood-in-history-risks-knocking-canadian-economy-off-course/). The *Calgary Herald* noted that $9.2 million was spent on mental

health support for the thousands traumatized by the event (http://
www.calgaryherald.com/news/Province+spend+million+mental+he
alth+support+flood+victims/9084287/story.html). Yes, people were
laid low. But Alberta's oil reserves are the third largest in the world.
There is no shortage of capital to fund rebuilding. If it were just about
picking up the pieces and starting again, Calgarians would do it at
warp speed.

But it wasn't just about rebuilding. I visited Calgary several times
in the months following the flood, and I talked to ordinary folks about
climate-related disaster, the oilsands, sustainable consumption, the
works. These were friends and colleagues, people who would give
me candid answers. Their responses reflected an anxiety that comes
with getting your boat seriously rocked.

All of them—even those who made a living in the oil sector—recognized the reality of climate change. All of them acknowledged the
oilsands were bad for the environment. Most of them feared the flood
was just the harbinger of things to come.

And all of them asked me what the hell I would have them do
now—stop producing oil?

The reality is, they're right. Oil production isn't the problem (the
carnage being created by oil producers in northern Alberta notwith-
standing).

The real problem is that we feel we're connected to oil like Sia-
mese twins. Tear it away from us, and we die. Or, at the very least, we
go back to living in the trees.

Certainly, government timidity around replacing oil with renew-
able energy doesn't help. Neither do big oil lobbyists working over-
time to kill anything that threatens the flow of black gold. But the
root of the problem is our insatiable desire for more stuff, and the
terrible job marketers have done firing up our passion for environmentally smart products.

So it's easy to understand the mixed feelings Calgarians have about their status as oil producers. Just as it's easy to understand the anxiety they feel when they think of themselves as oil consumers. They're frustrated with the status quo, and they want change. But they're terrified of change, and they want the status quo.

Calgary provides just one example of the confusion consumers are feeling when it comes to their relationship with the environment. It's an interesting paradox that could be studied for years, if we had years to spare. But we don't. Marketers have to get into high gear now. Unfortunately, that's something that doesn't mesh well with slow-moving big brands.

TECH OD

We've established that our greed has brought us to the brink of financial ruin, and our hyperconsumption could trigger an environmental apocalypse.

Surely there's an app for that?

Sorry for the bad joke. But it does provide a nice segue to another phenomenon that is unnerving consumers.

Technology fuels innovation. And innovation fuels technology. Put them all together and you have a steady stream of "New and Improved" products to consume. (You also have the worst case of planned obsolescence imaginable, but I digress.)

As marketers, we've linked technological innovation to the promise of a better, safer, more convenient world, reassuring consumers that if there's something wrong, the R&D guys will figure out a way to solve it and package it to buy.

So where's the problem?

Just as consumption has gone hyper and planned obsolescence has rendered products passé before their paint is dry, technological innovation is outpacing our capacity to absorb it. This is leading to situations that are in some cases silly, in some cases sad, and in other cases disconcerting.

For example, we're stunting our ability to forge deep bonds with humans as we communicate more virtually, which is sad. And the companies offering us connections to virtual friends are gathering reams of our personal information in exchange—which is disconcerting.

It may be fiction, but David Egger's book *The Circle* provides a not-too-far-fetched vision of where this could lead (http://www.nytimes.com/2013/11/03/books/review/the-circle-by-dave-eggers.html). It begins with our protagonist landing her dream job at a company portrayed as the next iteration of Facebook. As the book progresses, she is pushed to live the company mantra of sharing her life online, all the time. She does so with gusto, even wearing a necklace camera that beams her unfiltered human interactions to legions of online "friends."

There's collateral damage to this always-on life—her parents are traumatized and her ex-boyfriend driven to suicide by the unblinking voyeurism. Even the company's founder, a hoodie-wearing Zuckerberg type, is neutralized by his partners in Stalinesque fashion when he tries to put the brakes on his transmogrifying creation. The story concludes with our protagonist, chirpy and unquestioning, welcoming us to the Brave New World Huxley envisioned (http://billmoyers.com/content/orwell-vs-huxley-who-are-you-behind/).

But that won't happen, right?

I'm not so sure. We're happy to exchange our personal information for the latest online distraction, and we don't blink at revealing intimate details to our virtual friends. Not surprisingly, online blackmail is thriving, although it hasn't yet been adopted by government as a tool for creating the next McCarthy purge. Not officially, anyway.

The government is, however, spying on our phone calls and social interactions en masse. God bless you, Edward Snowden.

It seems the only thing missing to make *The Circle*'s prophecy complete is a big company with incredible data-gathering skills, phenomenal innovation, and questionable motives.

Enter Google.

Not long ago, I read about the launch of blackout hoods for Google Glass eyewear (http://www.custom3dstuff.com/glasskap/). So now our few remaining real friends won't freak out thinking the camera is rolling every time we look at them. Phew, that's reassuring.

It kind of begs the question why I would put the glasses on in the first place. What exactly is Google doing with the video feed I *do* record and upload to my social sites?

In other news, both Google and Facebook are investing heavily in drone technology, which will enable them to see what we're doing in those rare moments when we aren't facedown in a screen or walking around with Google Glass eyewear. No matter what Amazon promises about using drones to deliver products wherever we are, I can't get past the idea that delivering data to Google is the endgame here.

Jim Gleick, author of "The Information," wraps it all up with a bow: "We've all learned that the nicest people with the best intentions are capable of bringing evil into the world. No matter how sincere and idealistic they are, they are concentrating an enormous amount of power in our informational universe in a very small number of hands. A single, giant company responsible only to its managers can't claim to have the world's interests at heart. Ultimately, what Google does is for Google." (http://www.amazon.ca/The-Information-History-Theory-Flood/dp/1400096235)

Doesn't make you want to jump up and bake a cake, does it?

Personally, I see three possible outcomes here.

First, we'll snap out of it, just like we snapped out of other aberrations like TV dinners and accountants on Harleys. We'll begin to realize our screen friends have nothing on the real friend sitting across the table, and we don't need a drone watching over us. I believe this is the most likely scenario, as the pendulum swings back and we realize that companies offering friendship for a click are just plain creepy.

Perhaps hinting at this, a bathroom ad I saw in a local Canadian bar a while back urged patrons to turn off their phones and have some real interaction while at the bar. As cynical as this effort might sound—the ad was sponsored by a telecommunications provider and felt a bit like cigarette companies urging us not to smoke—I believe it speaks volumes about the backlash the telco's fear as people get satiated on social media.

On the grassroots side, you see movements like National Unplugging Day urging people to observe the principles of the Sabbath (rule number one: avoid technology) once a year (http://sabbathmanifesto. org/). Thinking we can manage only one day a year without our virtual friends is depressing. But hey, it's a start.

If that doesn't happen, there's always scenario two. The next generation, in time-honored fashion, will rebel against their parents—this time by embracing a nonvirtual life. Mom, Dad, we're Amish, or something to that effect. Actual fact—the Amish faith is one of the fastest-growing religions in North America. I kid you not. (http:// www.dailymail.co.uk/news/article-2187733/Amish-fastest-growing-religious-groups-US.html.)

The final, most likely scenario is that things will stay on the same track, aided and abetted by technological innovation. If this is the case, I foresee increasingly bland future consumers. We'll be afraid of putting ourselves "out there" where we might embarrass ourselves. We'll become even more voyeuristic and narcissistic. No more Just Doing It. No more Thinking Different. Instead, a world of Gap chinos and Brooks Brothers button-downs (kinda like a trip to P&G's Cincinnati headquarters, come to think of it). Irish pubs around the world will close. We'll all behave like squeaky-clean born-again Christian politicians. Yes, friends, a fate worse than death.

On the positive side, if that happens, all those annoying books on exploiting Big Data for better marketing will be useless. Our consumer data will be as predictable as pablum.

I'll happily grant these prognostications don't come from years of academic research. My predictions are based on news I absorb daily and my natural interest in connecting dots. Besides, there are too many X factors at play to make any credible academic predictions. Like a pinball, technological innovation can be thrown on a new track at any moment by disruptive events.

We may be able to dodge the dystopian future predicted by Eggers in *The Circle*. But, as marketers, we still have to deal with some very real conditions brought on by tech overload today. I want to highlight two of those conditions.

First, the Stupid Curve.

In 1965, Intel founder Gordon Moore predicted the number of transistors on integrated circuits would double every two years, thanks to the exponential nature of technological innovation. Moore got it right. Our computing power (and the wonderful new products it enabled) has accelerated like a car, then a plane, then a rocket. Dream it today—buy it tomorrow.

The only problem is, so many people are dreaming of cool things, and so many people are making those dreams real, that we're being flooded with amazing electronic tools, toys, and devices. And we have to learn how to use them.

As humans, we're used to learning curves. You get a new device, bumble along as you figure out how to make the damn thing do what it's supposed to, then start feeling smarter as you gain proficiency. Eventually, you reach the learning curve's peak. You're the king of the world and ready to take on another challenge.

But what if your device is rendered obsolete before you're halfway along the learning curve, and you're back to square one with the new version? Now multiply that by every device you own, every operating system you work with, and every app people say you simply can't live without.

Suddenly one little learning curve becomes a tidal wave of curves that buries you. Too many improvements to absorb, too many updates to install, too many new ways to get the old job done. You've been sentenced to life as a newbie, feeling perennially stupid and incompetent. Worse still, you can't stop the train and get off, for fear of being left behind in the Luddite dust.

Which leads us to the next source of anxiety—cognitive overload.

As technology author Nicholas Carr writes in his book *The Shallows,* "Psychologists refer to the information flowing into our working memory as our cognitive load. When the load exceeds our mind's ability to process and store it, we're unable to retain the information or to draw connections with other memories. We can't translate the new material into conceptual knowledge. Our ability to learn suffers, and our understanding remains weak." (http://www.theshallowsbook.com/nicholascarr/Nicholas_Carrs_The_Shallows.html)

What ensues is cognitive overload.

Essentially, cognitive overload decreases our capacity to learn new things. So being overloaded with technology updates hinders our ability to master those updates.

But decreased learning capacity and attention span aren't the only symptoms. Cognitive overload affects our moods, our sleep, everything. It makes us sick.

Now the unsurprising news. We are in a state of cognitive overload nearly every day. As Tony Schwartz, workplace efficiency expert, writes, "Far and away the biggest work challenges most of us now face are cognitive overload and difficulty focusing on one thing at a time" (http://dealbook.nytimes.com/2013/05/17/faced-with-overload-a-need-to-find-focus/?_php=true&_type=blogs&_r=0).

Schwartz's claim is backed by numbers. "Dying for Information," a Reuters study of more than a thousand junior, middle, and senior managers in the United Kingdom, United States, Singapore, Hong Kong, and Australia (http://old.cni.org/regconfs/1997/ukoln-content/repor~13.html) relays the following:

- Two-thirds of managers reported tension with work colleagues and loss of job satisfaction because of stress associated with information overload.

- One-third of managers (and 43 percent of senior managers) suffered from ill health brought on by stress associated with information overload.

- 62 percent of managers testified their personal relationships suffered as a direct result of information overload.

- 43 percent of managers thought important decisions were delayed, and their ability to make important decisions was affected, as a result of having too much information.

Now for the disturbing bit. This study was done in 1997. The good old days, before social media, 4G, apps. Anyone feeling cognitive overload today would look back at 1997 with nostalgia.

Of course, we'll adapt to cognitive overload, just as we adapted in 1997. But what form will our adaptation take?

If current indicators bear out, we'll become a more superficial, reactive, frazzled population. We'll blink, not think.

Combine this with our greater voyeuristic, narcissistic tendencies, and what do you have? A world of five-year-olds with too much sugar in them. Yay.

So back to the opening thought of this section. There may well be an app to help us get past hyperconsumption and environmental destruction.

But are you going to ask consumers to take the time to figure it out?

CULTURE CHAOS

I've touched on the economic, environmental, and technological trials our fitful times have foisted upon us. It seems only right to finish on a force created by all of the above—culture chaos.

Culture for people is a bit like water for fish. Most of us don't know we have one, although we plainly see cultural biases in those *outside* our group—biases that stop them from seeing the world as it *really* is.

Our culture is key to our identity. The group we belong to influences what we perceive as cool or nerdy, de rigueur or verboten. Our brand preferences are very much connected to our culture.

Thriving cultures are built on a solid foundation of shared values, and a steady inflow of new ideas. Stem the flow of ideas, and the culture stagnates. Allow a tidal wave of ideas, and you risk instability.

In an increasingly wired world, it's nearly impossible to block new ideas from outside. Certainly, oppressive regimes like North Korea's do their best, but they're an anomaly. And from the accounts I've read, it hasn't helped them create a terribly healthy, dynamic culture.

The nice thing about today's technology-driven inflow is that it can be regulated by controlling our screen time. In theory at least, we can absorb new ideas at our own speed, without going catatonic from cognitive overload.

On the horizon, however, I see tidal waves of new that can't be turned off. They won't come to us on screens, but in the form of hordes of people from far-off places. The cause of these tidal waves will be migration driven by climate change, and the economic chaos it engenders.

Humans have migrated since, well, forever. We've moved for a myriad of reasons—following the seasons, chasing the herds, escaping from one nastiness or another. In short, seeking a better life.

Major migrations triggered by economic, political, and natural disruptions are nothing new, either—think Irish Potato Famine, the Great Depression, and pretty much every major conflict since ancient times. So what makes these new migrations so different?

For one, the numbers are getting bigger.

During the dirty thirties, 2.5 million Americans abandoned their dustbowl farms and headed west.

In 2009, the UN High Commissioner for Refugees estimated

36 million people had been displaced by natural disasters and climate change.

In 2012, an Asian Development Bank report estimated 42 million people were displaced by climate-related disasters in *Asia alone* (http://www.adb.org/news/climate-linked-migration-poses-growing-humanitarian-threat-study).

Now scientists predict the number of climate refugees could hit 200 million by 2050 (http://education.nationalgeographic.com/education/encyclopedia/climate-refugee/?ar_a=1).

That's a problem, considering Earth is getting crowded. Refugees can't simply uproot and stake a new claim in terra nova. They've got to squeeze into places that are already bursting at the seams, probably facing their own climate-related strains, and not feeling terribly neighborly.

Thankfully, it won't happen tomorrow. Rising sea levels will take years to swamp Bangladesh (http://www.sciencedirect.com/science/article/pii/S2212096313000003X), and California still has water left. Climate change is gradual, producing a steady stream of migrants whose numbers can, with some foresight, be absorbed and assimilated.

Climate-related *disasters*, however, are a different animal. When they hit hard enough and often enough to overwhelm infrastructure and support systems, people pack up and leave. Fast.

A year after Hurricane Katrina, for example, the worst-hit Louisiana counties had lost 385,000 people, or 39 percent of their *total population*, to migration. That despite state infrastructure to help the afflicted stay and rebuild their homes.

The bad news is, we're in for more hurricanes, more tornadoes, more of all the variations on the "Mother Nature isn't happy" theme. Between 2000 and 2009, there were three times more climate-related disasters than there were between 1980 and 1989, according to the *New England Journal of Medicine* (http://www.nejm.org/doi/full/10.1056/nejmra1109877?query=featured_home&). Google climate trends, and you'll see this stat isn't an anomaly. Track the rising economic costs of rebuilding after these disasters, and you'll see it isn't financially sustainable, either.

I think we've had the smallest taste of migrations to come. Climate scientists agree on a steady rise in climate-related disasters and have put big circles around the global areas expected to take the worst hit (FYI, Asia is ground zero). But nobody can predict exact events, when they'll strike, where, how badly, if they'll lead to infrastructure collapse, and how many people they'll send packing. There are simply too many X factors at play.

We can, however, get a glimmer of the *cultural chaos* these global migrations could create. There are phenomena that mirror, in a small way, the effects we're expecting if mass migrations become the norm. One example is international tourism.

Mass migrations and large-scale tourism do have a few things in common. A large number of people entering a region. A local host who needs to accommodate the masses. And an ebb and flow in numbers that can reflect refugees being processed to other countries or tourists leaving in low season.

The UN studied the effect of tourist "tidal waves" to destinations, and discovered four ways that local cultures were being knocked off their foundations (http://www.unep.org/resourceefficiency/business/ sectoralactivities/tourism/factsandfiguresabouttourism/impactsof- tourism/socio-culturalimpacts/negativesocio-culturalimpactsfrom- tourism/tabid/78781/default.aspx):

1. Commodification: Local rituals, practices, and sites are sanitized and commoditized to make them palatable to visitors in what is called "reconstructed ethnicity." As a result, they lose their sacred or unique value to locals.

2. Standardization: Tourists may come for a new experience, but they crave products they're familiar with. Fast-food restaurants

and international hotel chains, for example.

3. Loss of authenticity and staged authenticity: Local practices, dress, and rituals are reconstructed for tourists. Like commodification, this robs the local culture of its authenticity and devalues it in the eyes of the locals.

4. Adaptation to tourist demands: Local artisans are tapped to create artifacts that satisfy tourist tastes. Although it gives the artisans a sense of worth, cultural erosion results from the commodification.

This rings true, you might say, but only in the case of wealthy tourists "invading" poorer countries and using their dollars to unwittingly maim the local culture. Not so. Consider the cultural imbroglio created by Euro Disney:

"Resistance in France has come from various constituencies. French intellectuals declared themselves against the very idea of a Disney park which is openly propagandistic in content and practice. The French government made specific requirements to ensure a degree of Europeanization of the park, and the employees and the public has done the rest. Two years into the park's operations, it consistently failed to meet operating costs. It is not clear that the failure had to do with the public's specific dislike of the park's attractions, but what is clear is that neither the government nor the people were ready to tolerate an exclusive enclave, with its own rules and social customs. But whereas the Government put its emphasis on political symbols and the economic revenues, the employees and the public worried about accessibility and exclusion, autonomy, hierarchy and jurisdiction over the public realm" (http://aei.pitt.edu/7021/1/spinelli_maria-lydia.pdf).

One might also consider the reaction of wealthy Hong Kong residents to the tidal wave of mainland Chinese flooding the city:

"Tourism has become a boon to the local economy, with visitors contributing more than 5 percent of the city's GDP last year, yet it has started to put pressure on Hong Kong's local community. The effects of the influx of tourists go even deeper than bad behavior—the spending preferences of mainland visitors have altered the city's urban fabric and triggered feelings among locals that their culture and way of life are under threat" (http://www.huffingtonpost.com/2013/11/20/chinese-tourists-hong-kong_n_4298781.html).

It's less about rich people foisting their culture onto poor people than it is about sheer numbers of outsiders threatening to overwhelm the local culture.

While unrelenting migrations caused by climate disasters haven't happened yet, all indicators say they will. And the sheer numbers of migrants could conceivably unsettle, or even trample, the culture of host countries. What then?

I predict three outcomes.

Homogenization

Euro Disney attempted a mash-up of French culture and American fantasy, creating a bland, homogenized picture everyone could digest. In the same way, both hosts and migrants could find the interesting, unique elements of their cultures washed away as everyone struggles to get along.

Hostility

As local cultures are overwhelmed, hosts will likely feel threatened. They'll become hyperprotective of icons and rituals they hold dear. Unfortunately, this will likely kill the inflow of new ideas, causing the culture to calcify and stagnate.

Disconnection

Possibly the greatest damage will be the disconnection of generations. Young people—both hosts and refugees—will more readily embrace the new, and older people will cling to their own culture for comfort. This will spark generational conflict and alienation.

As a marketer, this is all uncharted territory.

We could jump to obvious solutions—perhaps global brands will pull everyone together, so we can buy the world a Coke and keep it company. But this paints a superficial picture and ignores the complexity, confusion, and emotional charge of the situation.

We can segregate brands, making it about us versus them. But does this leave us stuck in time, unable to morph as the cultures evolve (or devolve)?

Or we can keep an open mind, reminding ourselves this disorder is the new world order, and chaos is the source of incredible innovation. Precisely the sort of innovation that could help us create brands that work.

PART II.

CREATING THE FUTURE:

HAVING DESCRIBED A STRANGE NEW WORLD, WE EXPLORE HOW TO MAKE A GO OF MARKETING IN IT.

BREATHE

EMBRACE YOUR CLUELESS
(THANK YOU, JOHN MARSHALL ROBERTS)

I've always been a sponge for new ideas. Maybe it's a lateral think-ing thing. Maybe ADD.

I get waylaid in library aisles and bookstores, spend hours at mag-azine racks, and search online like a kid on a museum field trip—con-stantly wandering off to poke the dinosaur and honk the horn of the antique car.

I'm a sucker for new thinking, even if it has nothing to do with the job at hand. Actually, *especially* if it has nothing to do with the job at hand. I have a soft spot in my heart for topics I'm woefully underinformed on. Meeting experts in other fields fires me up like a shot of sugar.

The only downside is that all this activity leaves me feeling like the dumbest guy in the room. Why do so many people know so much more than me? How am I going to learn all this stuff, and the stuff I haven't even discovered yet? How do I incorporate all these ideas into what I do, without spinning off course? And most important, how the heck do I make money at it?

John Marshall Roberts, the behavioral psychologist I introduced you to earlier, seemed familiar with my dilemma and offered a solution. He said I should embrace my inner clueless.

"I'm seeing the rise of systems thinkers—people trying to make sense of how *everything* works and hangs together. They're specialists, but somewhere along the line they realized what they know is insignificant in the grand scheme of things. They're having their brains blown by the magnitude of it all. The successful ones accept the concept of being a perennial beginner, abandoning their illusions of expertise."

The whole thing feels like a Zen concept because it is a Zen concept. It's called Beginner's Mind. Zen teacher Shunryu Suzuki summarized it: "In the beginner's mind there are many possibilities, in the expert's mind there are few."(http://www.arvindguptatoys.com/arvindgupta/zenmind.pdf)

The key word here is *possibilities*. When it comes to solutions for global problems (and how to market them effectively), there are myriad solutions. But our expertise has made us more adept at criticizing new solutions than promoting them.

Accept conventional North American wisdom on climate change, for example, and you accept our only option is to drive the planet into a brick wall. This crash comes with the official-sounding title "climate adaptation."

Yes, we need to adapt as Mother Nature exacts her revenge for our profligate behavior. But climate adaptation feels more and more like the only option being seriously proffered. Any open-minded beginner could tell you this isn't the only possibility. In fact, it's a lousy, stunted way forward.

On the same subject, we marketers tend to accept a rather limited role in mitigating climate change. We've become experts in selling the products our clients tell us to sell. Our expertise has constrained our vision of the possible. We've become order takers, thinking our creativity needs to be confined to the 5 Ps. In a world where linear production and hyperconsumption are major problems, throwing up our hands and saying it's not our department is both a great shame and a missed opportunity for creative thinking.

Why do we keep doing it, then?

I think it comes down to a society that hasn't yet come around to embracing its inner clueless, instead putting too much emphasis on the opinions of gurus.

BEWARE THE GURU

We used to refer to Ron Woodall, one of the driving creative forces behind the rise of Palmer Jarvis Advertising, as our ad-Yoda. He didn't entirely detest the moniker, because it inferred wisdom without ego. Also, Yoda was weird and talked funny, which Ron liked.

Ron did, however, hate being called a guru. The whole all-knowing wise man vibe really rubbed him the wrong way. I recall someone introducing him as an ad guru at a Palmer Jarvis event. Ron got on the microphone and said, "Ad guru? If I'm a guru, I guess I must be dead, then."

I've met people in my business who, unlike Ron, have an affinity for the term, who use it to describe themselves, who actually print it on their business cards. There are a few reasons why, if you ever meet these people, you should run away.

The term *guru* implies spiritual enlightenment. This is ridiculous when you apply it to advertising or marketing. We sell stuff like pimple cream and chain saws, not salvation.

A bigger problem is that gurus are expected to have definitive answers. That's possible with a subject where nothing new is happening. Ancient Babylonian architecture or Sherlock Holmes stories, for example. It's conceivable you could learn everything there is to know there and attain guru status.

But marketing deals with human psychology, which is a never-ending story. You can't be a guru in a subject that's open-ended and constantly surprising us with new twists and turns.

The biggest problem, though, is that the term *guru* sounds smug. Smugness is bad. Smugness inhibits your ability to absorb new ideas. Smug people consider it an insult when someone challenges their authority. Even worse, when your smug assertions are upended—as they invariably will be—people will take great pleasure in taping "kick me" signs to your backside.

That's why you shouldn't aspire to guru-dom. Of course, we all do it. Nobody wants to be constantly questioning, tearing down, and rebuilding. It gives us migraines. Once we climb a mountain of learning, we want to rest on our laurels a bit.

And let's not forget people *want* gurus. We want direction, black-and-white answers, and clear instruction from authority figures. When a climate scientist tells us hurricanes may or may not be directly linked to climate change, we boo and tell him to come back with something solid. When Angela Merkel tells us Austerity is the *only* way out of Europe's economic quagmire, we want to believe her. She's a PhD, she's German, and her nickname is "the Decider." She's got guru written all over her.

Lobbyists and marketers understand this. That's why we say, with the passion of a Southern Baptist minister, that coal is clean, tightening our belts will solve fiscal irresponsibility, and eyeglasses with cameras will make us sexy.

Passion, even when it's backed by superficial or wrong facts, works.

So how do we, as marketers, shift from selling superficial sound bites to selling the infinitely more complex truth?

I'm no guru. I can't claim to have the patented, 100 percent guaranteed, endorsed by Warren Buffett solution. But I do have thoughts to share. And they just might work for you.

Here goes.

WHAT DO YOU STAND FOR?

THE STORY OF CHIPPER (THANK YOU, PATAGONIA)

A few years back, I attended a Conscious Capitalism brainstorm at the Ventura, California, headquarters of Patagonia.

Patagonia is an incredible company. Founded by Yvon Chouinard as a means to supply himself and his "dirtbag climber" friends with quality equipment, it has grown into a global brand without sacrificing its environmental, design, quality, or ethical business ideals.

As part of my visit, I did a tour and met some of the employees. I have never come across a more enthusiastic, intelligent, genuine, committed bunch. These guys were off the proverbial charts. I was awed, I felt envious, I began to suspect some kind of smart and happy juice in the water supply.

Even in that group of cheerful overachievers, one person stood out. Chipper Bell, our guide for the company tour.

Chipper bore more than a passing resemblance to the Dude in *The Big Lebowski*, from his insanely laid-back demeanor and Jeff Bridges looks to his cartoon California accent.

As he toured us through the company, however, it became apparent there was more to Chipper than met the eye.

Passing through the materials research department, we ducked as someone flipped a Frisbee to Chip, calling out that his design had finally arrived.

Chipper was ecstatic, explaining to us that this disk was created using recycled materials and sustainable processes. After a bit of back patting, one of us asked why creating a sustainable Frisbee was such a big deal for him. Chipper replied with Dude nonchalance that he was a Frisbee freestyle world champion, shrugged his shoulders, and ushered us on.

We were still digesting this nugget when Chipper opened the door to the stairwell where employees stashed their surfboards. He pointed out his board and explained that anyone at Patagonia could skip out to surf when nearby breaks were pumping, as long as they got their work done later. Again, one of us piped up and asked what Chipper loved most about surfing. He replied that he ran a surf school when he wasn't at Patagonia, and he was most inspired by his special-needs and disabled students.

Again, we were stunned into silence. Who was this Dude?

The tour ended as Chip took us to his desk and told us what he did at Patagonia. Turns out he wasn't in community relations, product research, or sustainability, as I had imagined.

He was Patagonia's receptionist.

As he put on his headset and cheerfully waved good-bye, I discreetly asked one of our Patagonia hosts to give me the full Chipper story.

"Did he tell you he almost got to run the company?" My host smiled.

"No, he left that one out" I said, picking my jaw up off the ground.

Turns out there was a companywide vote a few years back to elect a new president. Chipper came in a close second. Our Frisbee champion, surf school owner, Dude receptionist had come a hairbreadth from running Patagonia.

Know what? He probably would've been a great president. Perhaps a bit shy on management theory, but no more so than half the presidents out there.

I'd argue, however, that Chip would've been wasted as president. The role he had now was of far greater importance. More than any brand, any communications campaign, any iconic image, he *represented* Patagonia.

When I think of Chip, and the other people I've met at Patagonia these past years, I get a crystal clear picture of what the company represents. Its values and motives, what it will always make and never make, how it will behave in good times and bad. I feel aligned with Patagonia, much like I'd feel aligned with a trusted friend. We *get* each other.

Interestingly, Patagonia rarely advertises. Yet it attracts a legion of loyal followers who support it in good times and bad. Its sales actually went up in the last recession, without price cuts.

I'm sure every marketer would like to know how to pull that rabbit out of the Gore-Tex hat.

BRANDS DON'T HAVE BELIEFS—PEOPLE DO

I think the secret is standing in front of us. It's people.

If I was to use Chip as a model, I'd say the secret is people who are remarkable, attract other people, and cheerfully express their honest beliefs in the products they make. Their "advertising" is the stories they share when customers come shopping.

You find these people everywhere, working for great companies. Nordstrom, lululemon, Interface carpet.

The trick is, these people and their very genuine stories can't be invented. Marketers can't fabricate beliefs or values.

Of course, that doesn't stop us from trying. I know from personal experience.

When my team was assigned the task of reviving the Mr. Clean brand, we began by digging into its past marketing. Our head office and P&G happily complied with our requests for vintage material, sending us Mr. Clean ad campaigns that went back to the black-and-white days.

Then one morning, a manila envelope landed on my desk. It was the story of Mr. Clean himself.

To be clear, this wasn't a description of how the icon was originally designed by P&G and its ad agency. It was a bona fide biography, starting at Mr. Clean's birth (discovered on the doorstep by his adoptive Midwest parents) to his present-day life (traveling the world on a permanent cleaning tour of duty). It was flowing prose. It was inspiring. It was insane.

I read it, then passed it to the team working on the Mr. Clean account, and they read it. We stared at each other, dumbstruck.

"Isn't this guy a cartoon?"

"Who the heck got paid to do this?"

"Mr. Clean had parents? He was a sailor? WTF?"

The overriding reaction was that someone was pulling our leg. Or, if this was in fact a serious effort at building the brand, it was misguided and creepy.

We kept the document to ourselves, trusting consumers would greet a "serious" biography of a cleaning-bottle icon with confusion and cynical derision, as we had.

Now, years later, it seems another team of marketers begs to differ. The agency that currently holds the Mr. Clean account released a commercial devoted to the icon's "life" (http://www.adweek.com/news/advertising-branding/ad-day-mr-clean-150292).

The ad, shot like a blockbuster trailer, starts with Mr. Clean as a child, polishing the house with his mom. Then on to college, where he unravels complex cleaning formulas with a professor. He travels the world. He hugs sailors. He studies cleaning at a Shaolin kung fu monastery. He wanders alone from town to town, helping everyone from Grandma to the short-order cook get their counters clean—an unsung hero with obsessive-compulsive disorder.

The ad confirms my hunch. To paraphrase one of the comments on YouTube, it is sadly not intentionally funny.

Certainly, the agency could say it was done on a lark, all tongue in cheek. From my experience with Procter, I'd say that story wouldn't pass the sniff test. Procter doesn't do anything "on a lark." Somewhere between that proverbial tongue and cheek is a very serious attempt to fuse human personality onto a corporate entity. An expensive attempt, judging from the high production values and prime media buy (the spot aired, for example, on big screens in conjunction with the launch of the latest Superman movie). Any commercial with that price tag wasn't done for a laugh.

What I suspect is that the Mr. Clean team created the biography commercial because they knew what Patagonia knows. Humans forge stronger bonds than ad campaigns.

Ad campaigns can't create the deep, trusting relationships that humans can. They don't have human belief systems and values. Instead, they serve up a concoction of emotional hooks and superficial promises, hoping to leave us with a positive feeling when we hear the brand mentioned or see it on the shelf.

This worked like a charm in simpler, pre-www days. But the world has evolved and become more hostile to ad campaigns. We're oversaturated with media. People simply don't have the bandwidth to absorb any more vapid brand hooks. And today's consumer has the ability to look behind the curtain and see how the brand behaves when it isn't trying to ingratiate itself. Stories of sweatshop labor, disregard for the environment, and sociopathic pursuit of profit don't jibe terribly well with a warm and cuddly image.

Not surprisingly, trust in brands has gone down the toilet. As Havas Media's Meaningful Brands study points out, most people worldwide wouldn't care if 73 percent of brands disappeared tomorrow.

In North America, that number is closer to 92 percent (http://www.havasmedia.com/meaningful-brands). As Umair Haque, the study's author, writes:

> The long-standing relationship between people and brands is broken. Much of the trust, respect and loyalty people had for many brands has disintegrated.
>
> You see it every day in the level of cynicism, scepticism and indifference that people have toward many brands, in many interactions. The reality is, trust in brands worldwide has been falling for the last three decades. It is not hard to see why. We have faced the greatest financial recession since the great depression. It is a recession that hangs on stubbornly in much of the world, with a sluggish rebound at best.
>
> Then there is the fact that brands are not delivering what people want. Instead, they're trying to deliver what they always have: the same old combination of faster/cheaper/newer, while the world yearns for brands that are meaningful. Brands that improve people's well-being in a tangible, significant, fulfilling way.

So let's circle back to my question at the close of the last section—why doesn't Patagonia feel the need to advertise?

Haque has the answer. Successful brands provide meaning, not superficial promises. They "advertise" by building human bonds, providing reliability and utility, behaving like trustworthy people would. People we like, admire, and want to emulate.

This isn't done with thirty-second spots or billboards. It's done when people like me tell people like you about people like Chipper Bell, Patagonia's receptionist.

I believe the best brands *are* people. They just happen to be associated with products or services.

YOU CAN'T INVENT MEANING

Not every company has leaders like Patagonia's Yvon Chouinard or receptionists like Chipper Bell. Does that mean they can't succeed?

Nothing could be further from the truth.

What a brand must have, however, is *authentic* meaning. Meaning that comes from the vision of the founders. What were they thinking when they decided to create this product or service? How did they see it improving people's lives, and changing their world?

This, I suspect, is where Mr. Clean's attempts at creating deeper relationships with consumers falters. Look behind the icon and the product, and you see a group of well-intentioned, nice people at Procter who do a great job, sell lots, and make shareholders happy, but simply aren't motivated by a sense of meaning. They know *what* they're doing, but don't know *why*.

You can't invent meaning for a brand. It's like trying to invent yourself. Certainly, you can change your town, your friends, your look. You can tweak your résumé to make it more impressive. But fabricating what you stand for, what you value, your essence, is a recipe for disaster. This is core stuff that defines who you are.

People can smell brands with no meaning or fabricated meaning. Even if they're dressed in cool design and say all the right things, they lack character and act without a moral compass. These brands, like their sociopathic human kin, end up being guided solely by pursuit of profit. Inevitably, this leads to nasty headlines about unethical behavior and crippling damage to the brand.

Happily, it doesn't have to be this way. Avoiding it isn't even that hard.

THE BRAND COMPASS

Most clients come to me with a brand in transition. They're launching it, just bought or inherited it, or want to overhaul it because it's getting hammered by competitors.

No matter the situation, our engagement generally starts the same way: creating a Brand Compass.

The Compass exercise gets to the heart of the brand, defining its story, essence, values, philosophy, how it walks and talks. It's called a compass because it gives direction, but could just as well be called a North Star, bible, or playbook.

Clients emerge from the exercise with visions of what their brands are, and what they can become. They also get a book with lots of cool photos to accompany the text (nobody wants to hear me labor through a thousand words when a great photo will do the trick). As soon as it's done, the book is usually tapped to inspire ad campaigns and design projects, but it's been used for everything from guiding hiring practices to investor presentations. I've even seen clients turn Brand Compasses into coffee-table books for their reception.

Where does the content come from? Some clients think I just wander their halls a bit, then pull it out of a hat. In truth, I get it much the same way my old boss Ron Woodall did when he was engineering the transformation of Palmer Jarvis. Ron simply sat down with people who gave a damn, he shut up, and he let them talk. Invariably, the brand spilled out.

It worked for Ron. It works for me.

I do the listening in a couple of phases. First, I conduct some (usually informal) research, chatting with people who give a damn. Then I take the core team through brainstorms.

I want to talk for a moment about the groups I conduct the initial research with, giving you a glimmer into their idiosyncrasies. Understand the quirks, and you get a much better end product.

They tend to fall into the following groups:

- The folks who run the company
- The folks who work at the company
- Customers

- Stakeholders
- Competitors
- The world

The Folks Who Run the Company

This group usually starts by sharing the lofty corporate mission with me. *We're people who sell people to people,* or something akin to that. Sometimes they've had the statement art directed into posters and hung around the office.

After showing deference to the brilliance of their mission statement, I gently redirect them, asking them things like why the heck they joined the company in the first place, and what drives them nuts. Sometimes they give me the autopilot press-sanitized answers, sometimes they stare like deer in the headlights, and sometimes they try to throw me off with alpha dog answers: "I joined because it put me in a new tax bracket" or "It makes me nuts that I only get the company jet twice a year."

At that point I just smile, sit, and stare at them. Invariably, like perps on *Law & Order*, they break down and spill.

These tend to be great chats, giving me a wealth of 35,000-foot overviews of the company and brand. Sometimes the material is a bit bloodless and intellectual, but sometimes it's pure gold. Letting people know you're there to listen seems to open repositories of thoughts that otherwise get squelched because they could be seen as too radical or silly.

The Folks Who Work at the Company

I speak with representatives from each department—marketing, operations, finance, sales, R&D, and the rest. Their responses tend to add color and dimension to the picture management painted for me.

There are two groups of employees I find particularly interesting. The people who work the call center and the self-appointed "big dogs".

The call center folks are the ones who deal with irate customers. Not only do they have the funniest stories, but they give me all the material I need to deflate puffery that may arise later. Without fail, they also provide the building blocks for genuine improvements that make the brand more powerful.

Pound for pound, though, the big dogs give the greatest entertainment.

In different companies, they inhabit different departments. On one particular project—the creation of a unified brand for two newly merged mutual fund companies—the big dogs were the individual fund managers.

In the course of interviews with each of the managers, I asked what their superpower was. Every man jack of them (there were no women—another characteristic of big dog groups) said they did exhaustive homework before investing. Then, each one of them looked around to make sure nobody was eavesdropping, and whispered loudly that he was the only one who did this deep research. The other guys just got by on luck.

They were fun interviews.

We built a platform on the new brand's commitment to research. Every fund manager thought I'd pulled it directly from his interview. The big dogs felt vindicated, they pulled together as a team, and the brand was a success.

Customers

Before I talk about what customers bring to the Brand Compass party, let me distinguish between B2B (business to business) customers and B2C (business to consumer) customers. They are very different animals.

B2B companies have fewer customers. The salespeople have them in their address books. So does the president, the service manager, someone in finance, and whoever takes care of restaurant reservations and free hockey tickets. Relationships are chummy, so it's tricky getting these customers to spill the beans. Conversely, if company and customer aren't feeling the love, forget about getting an interview. Who would want some consultant calling their irate customer to chat about brand strengths?

When the stars are aligned, however, B2B customers provide big insights. They're insider and outsider rolled into one. They understand the product, the personalities, the company, and all the other bits of the mix.

Just don't go expecting them to wax poetic on the brand. These folks pride themselves on buying based on product attributes and service. It's their job. Inferring they're influenced by a commercial or print ad only gets you dead air on the other end of the phone.

Now let's shift gears. B2C customers don't know the company president, they don't get spiffed hockey tickets, and they don't buy the product for a living. In fact, their interest in the brand usually comes down to recognizing the logo and maybe looking at the product in a store a few times a year. Maybe.

There's also a zillion of them, which means you have to leave the question asking to a research house. If you've ever done a research house interview, you probably concur this approach kills spontaneity and insights and instead provides mind-numbingly general statements.

If you opt to interview a small cross section of consumers yourself instead of taking the "spray and pray" approach, which small cross section do you talk to? I've spoken to folks who love the brand, folks who love the competitor's brand, and folks who think brands come on the rumps of cattle. What they all tend to have in common is a very, very general knowledge of the brand in question. No deep insights in that department.

What consumers do provide, though, is a healthy dose of humble pie. You begin to understand from talking to them that your project, your client's brand, the center of your universe, doesn't count for bubkes to consumers. In fact, the only time they care is if the product performed admirably for them, if someone they respect recommended it to them, or, of course, if the product didn't live up to the brand promise. Everybody remembers that.

Net net? Save your ad budget, and invest it in innovation and cultivating deeper human relationships.

Stakeholders

These are people who have a stake in the brand or company. Either they've invested financially (technically making them shareholders, but you get the drift), or they've invested emotionally.

There are some ground-shaking stakeholders out there, particularly those with a strong ethical stance on the company's doings. NGOs and activists regularly push companies to massive about-faces on sustainability and social equity. They're the antidote to Milton Friedman's depressing belief that the only social responsibility of a business is to increase its profits. In most cases, their interventions make companies stronger, workers happier and healthier, and brands more attractive.

Speaking with them is inspiring. They think in terms of possibilities. This provides an interesting dynamic. People "inside" the company tend to speak with caveats—"We want to improve this, but we tried it before and the boss's wife didn't like it." Outsiders aren't privy to all the reasons something won't work. They push hard for change.

When I speak with stakeholders, I get a great vision of what the company could become. This provides material for creating the brand's North Star vision—the dream that will guide the company's actions and aspirations forever, but will never be reached. Terrific stuff.

Competitors

Competitors all want to hear what we're up to and are happy to chat. Big surprise.

When I speak with them, I keep things broad and general. What's their perspective on the category and consumers? What do they think my client is doing right (a few things) and doing wrong (lots of things)?

Even without digging into details, though, I can glean invaluable insights from competitor conversations. I find out if my client's problems are typical of the sector. I discover what "blue water" areas aren't being explored by anyone in the sector, and why not. If I do the interviews by actually walking into stores and speaking with staff, I can also bring shoppers into the chat, getting a mini-brainstorm going that can expose common complaints and unfulfilled wishes.

The World

No, I don't travel the world looking for trends in the sector. I let my friends in media do it for me.

First, editors. The beauty of contributing to a number of journals (I send stories to *Huffington Post*, *Fast Company*, *GreenBiz*, and *Sustainable Brands*, among others) is that you develop a relationship with editors. On occasion, this relationship can be leveraged to get their perspective on trends.

In addition to speaking with editors, I also chat with journalists specializing in the sector. Again, my history as a writer works like a kind of secret handshake here. We talk about our latest content, share tips, then dig into their area of expertise. As journalists, they pride themselves on doing good research for their stories, tapping a number of different sources, getting counterpoints to their points. In essence, they do everything I've tried to do in all my interviews. Speaking with them is a terrific way to give my hunches an acid test and spark new areas for exploration.

Of course, the media aren't the only folks I tap for global insights. I also dig into my search engines and hound friends in research to send me any omnibus studies they might be able to lay their hands on. Thank you all.

Brainstorming

I mentioned a few pages back that my Brand Compass exercise has two parts—first, up-front research, and then leading the core team in brainstorms to turn all our learnings, hunches, and instincts into a marvelous new brand. I've covered the research. Now a few words on the brainstorms.

Brainstorms are really, really hard.

You need to inspire a group—many of them cynics—to drop their inhibitions, think outside the box, and push hard for new thinking. I don't care what anybody says about pencil crayons, Slinkys, and bouncy balls to open up the participants' brains and get their innovation on—pulling truly new ideas out is painful.

I have three tips for anyone venturing into the brainstorm room as a freshman facilitator.

First, know 90 percent of the results before you ever start the brainstorm. I've made the mistake of going into brainstorms expecting the group to put together all the pieces. They didn't.

Now I work with my client liaison beforehand, putting together the core research findings in a form that takes us to the doorstep of the new brand. All the team has to do is turn the doorknob and, hey presto, they've done it! Back slapping all around.

Second, seed some ringers in the room. Noisy consumers. A journalist. A creative type or two who can throw insane ideas out there without any fear of reprisal. It will make everyone else feel it's OK to behave a bit funky.

By the same token, don't put the boss in the room. It will absolutely kill any creativity or risky thinking. Nobody wants their boss thinking their ideas are lame. The boss's creative ego can be assuaged by promising a private brainstorming to put the icing on the cake.

Third, don't expect genius to pop out and hug you. As one of my clients who has been through a number of brainstormings says, "I always tell my team not to be disappointed when they don't nail it in the session. Oftentimes they *have* nailed it, but it's still an unwieldy idea with a great idea hidden inside. So we all agree to walk away, think more about the idea we hate the least, and let it germinate in our imaginations for a few days after the session."

The idea they hate the least? I'm flattered.

Following the brainstorm, I collect all the information, write it down, try to connect the dots, edit, and inject a twist of creativity. The creative twist, which I use to turn good results into "something we've never seen before" results, is the only part of the exercise where I might tap my own ideas. But careful—it's the people in the company who will bring the brand to life. Hijacking their thoughts with my "creative twists" can actually be counterproductive.

The Finished Product

The end product of this labor of love is a simple document—*simple* being a key word here.

It starts with the story of the brand. If it's a new brand, this can include the inspiration behind it and the path it hopes to take in the future. If it's a merged brand or a brand in transition, the story digs into the spark that helped bring it to life in the first place.

Following the story, I try to distill everything down into a short, simple essence statement. What is the one thought that personifies the brand? Is it simple enough that anyone could understand it? Interesting enough that everyone would want to know more? And surprising enough that saying it would silence other conversations in the elevator?

Then it's on to the values and philosophy of the brand. It's critical to remember here, and throughout the document, that we're talking on a human level. I've seen some Brand Compass–like documents penned by management teams before, and they're as entertaining as business plans. If I'm listing the brand values, these are human values. And the philosophy of the brand should be something a person should be able to understand and embrace. If we expect people to live the brand, they have to be excited to read the Brand Compass.

After the story, the essence, the values, and the philosophy, each individual compass tends to follow its individual path, with sections that are relevant to specific clients. Some of those sections have included the following:

- Us versus them: A map of qualities our brand personifies and competitor brands personify.
- How we talk: Does our brand communicate like a twenty-five-year-old programmer, a wise grandmother, or an enlightened, open-minded doctor from Europe? Setting the tone of voice up front helps ensure that people down the road don't imbue the brand with their own voices.
- Our graphics, and why they look that way: The Brand Compass isn't a graphics style guide. But often clients include their new logo and brand colors in it, with brief explanations of how everything links back to the strategy and why it looks like it does.
- Our innovation style: A by-product of the compass exercise is a bucketload of cool innovation ideas. Listing some of these ideas gives the reader an idea of the way we want to develop the product to fulfill the brand vision.
- Where we are, where we'll be: Nobody comes to me with a brand that doesn't need improving. That's why we sometimes include a section highlighting what our brand does right and wrong now, and what it will be doing better in the foreseeable future.

So there you have it. The easy, step-by-step guide to creating a Brand Compass and bringing your brand's essence to life. If you have any trouble creating your own, call me. I might be able to help you. But, more likely, I'll commiserate. Getting these things right is as painless as giving birth to a hippo.

CONNECTING ON A HIGHER LEVEL

AXE, DOVE, AND GROSS NATIONAL HAPPINESS

Axe body spray and deodorant runs ads promising teen boys an endless bevy of impossibly beautiful babes if they use the product.

Dove soap runs ads telling teen girls and women to feel good about themselves and reject the impossible feminine ideal served up by the beauty industry.

Now the punch line. Axe and Dove are owned by the same company, Unilever.

For the longest time, the hypocrisy of these contradictory messages wasn't a problem. Few people outside marketing knew Axe and Dove were owned by the same company. And those of us in marketing didn't see anything terribly deviant in the situation. Most of us promoted products that clashed ideologically—heck, I used to sell diet products in the morning and ice cream in the afternoon. Why couldn't Unilever sell two products to two different audiences with two very different messages?

In 2007, we found out why.

Someone created a video that patched a collage of sexy babe bits from Axe ads into a Dove commercial. The Dove spot, originally sporting the tagline "Talk to your daughter before the beauty industry does," suddenly had a new message: "Talk to your daughter before Unilever does" (http://www.youtube.com/watch?v=SwDEF-w4rJk&list=RDSwDEF-w4rJk).

The spot went viral. *Ad Age* covered it (http://adage.com/article/news/dove-viral-draws-heat-critics/122185/). Wolf Blitzer covered it (http://www.youtube.com/watch?v=dRNbZQ7K3vo). Hundreds of bloggers covered it. The social media world went into a lather over this one.

The marketing community was blindsided. All along we thought serving up a steady diet of "Buy this and you'll be more popular/sexy/you name it" would be enough to keep consumers happy. All those fiddly details behind the brand curtain—corporate ethics, for example—were a bore.

Turns out, the buying public weren't bored by ethics. In this case, they were incensed. They expected Unilever to behave with a conscience.

For the longest time, I thought this higher level of expectations was the result of consumers having their base needs satisfied. North Americans had become fairly prosperous (this was before the Great Recession, remember). We all smelled nice, drove nice cars, had nice clothes. This left us bored, and looking for something of a higher ethical order to buy into.

Then something crossed my radar that gave my theory the heave-ho. It was called the Gross National Happiness (GNH) index.

GNH was an official policy created in Bhutan to help citizens live, work, and consume in a way that aligned with their Buddhist spirituality. From the Bhutanese perspective, true prosperity could only occur when material and spiritual development happened side by side, complementing one another. As a result, the government implemented GNH, measuring not just economic growth but advancement in areas like sustainability, cultural values, good governance, and conservation of the natural environment. Turns out, it wasn't just North Americans who seemed to be looking for something more from their companies.

No formalized system like GNH had hit our shores. But I thought dots were being connected, a trend was taking shape, and people everywhere would inevitably start thinking beyond consumption.

I wasn't the only one connecting these dots. In 2008, the Legatum Institute created the first Global Prosperity Index (http://www.prosperity.com/#!/). Here's how they describe its mission:

> Traditionally, a nation's prosperity has been based solely on macroeconomic indicators such as a country's income, represented either by GDP or by average income per person (GDP per capita). However, most people would agree that prosperity is more than just the accumulation of material wealth, it is also the joy of everyday life and the prospect of being able to build an even better life in the future. The Prosperity Index is distinctive in that it is the only global measurement of prosperity based on both income and well-being.

Yes, economic indicators were part of the index. But so were measurements of well-being and life satisfaction like education, health, security, freedom, and governance.

And so, for me at least, began a new way of thinking about the people I was marketing to.

DUH, SAYS MASLOW

In 1943, Abraham Maslow wrote a paper titled "A Theory of Human Motivation" (http://www.simplypsychology.org/maslow.html). In essence, he said people were motivated to answer certain needs. When one need was satisfied, they moved on to the next.

Maslow mapped the needs out in a pyramid-shaped hierarchy, with the most basic (food, water, shelter) at the bottom; progressing to safety needs (protection and stability); then social needs (love, family, friends, a sense of belonging); esteem needs (prestige, achievement, independence); and finally self-actualization (personal growth, fulfillment, peak experiences).

Maslow posited that people were in a never-ending process of "becoming" more, always striving to move up the pyramid. However, only one in 150 ever reached the pyramid's peak of self-actualization. Others were held back by familiar roadblocks. They hit a rough patch like unemployment or divorce, for example, and had to refocus on basic needs like food, shelter, and security. They didn't feel their peer group would support them pushing higher. Or—and here's where it gets interesting—they were held in limbo at lower stages by society.

Wait, what sort of society would willingly impede its citizens on their journey to becoming happier, self-actualized people?

Our society.

I've spent the better part of my career convincing people that happiness lay just one purchase away. Buying the right brand would give them security, help them belong to a desirable social group, win prestige, and, yes, get them laid. Buying the wrong brand (or even worse, not buying) would invariably lead to banishment to the forest of ostracization.

In effect, a consumer society keeps its citizens in a state of arrested development, locked into a cycle of satisfying lower and midlevel needs. The last thing the people controlling our economy need is consumers questioning whether buying more products will actually make them happy. That's insurrection, amigo.

This status quo works for a time. But, as we're starting to see, the natives are getting restless. They want to think creatively, build a better world, question authority and societal norms, try new things instead of sticking to the safe option. The self-actualizers still want to buy, but they're putting a raft of new demands on brands. Authenticity, sustainability, social equity, and a sense of mission that transcends the product to what the brand stewards believe as humans.

Granted, not everyone wants to push the limits and become self-actualized. Many feel uncomfortable taking a new path, preferring to follow when things are safe. But those that are forging ahead have the power of social media in their hands to amplify their thoughts, questions, and challenges. The tiny group at the peak of the pyramid looks a lot bigger. This, conceivably, will accelerate the rate that followers jump aboard.

The Axe versus Dove debacle was a textbook case of self-actualizers challenging the rest of us to think more critically and perhaps, maybe, hopefully, make the world a bit better in the process. Since Axe versus Dove happened in 2007, we've become more acclimatized to whistleblowers calling recalcitrant brands to the carpet. Virtually every major North American brand has formed partnerships with NGOs to hold their feet to the fire. Leading brands like Patagonia go to great lengths to talk about the shortfalls in their production process, even inviting consumers to offer up ideas on how to make things better (http://www.patagonia.com/us/footprint/). Patagonia has also created a program whereby consumers can send in their old Patagonia gear for repair, eliminating the need to buy new stuff. It's a self-actualized company, and its fans are rewarding it with zealous loyalty and support.

And to think, Maslow saw it coming all along.

THE BOND OF SHARED BELIEF

Self-actualizers tend to be a pretty groovy crowd. They're the Lennons, Einsteins, Gandhis, and Picassos of the world. They make terrific role models. Advertisers love to wallow in their halo.

Companies led by self-actualized people also tend to stand out in the crowd. Patagonia is clearly one of those companies. Apple, at least under Steve Jobs, is another.

What I like about Apple's journey to self-actualization is that the company communicated it so damn well. For example, in perhaps the greatest paean to the twentieth century's giants of insight, intelligence, and creativity, Apple released a beautiful commercial called "Here's to the Crazy Ones" (http://www.youtube.com/watch?v=tjgtLSHhTPg). Over a collage of the best and brightest shot in black-and-white slo-mo, a simple voice-over read:

> Here's to the crazy ones. The misfits. The rebels. The trouble-makers. The round pegs in the square holes. The ones who see things differently. They're not fond of rules. And they have no respect for the status quo. You can quote them, disagree with them, glorify or vilify them. But the only thing you can't do is ignore them. Because they change things. They push the human race forward. And while some may see them as the crazy ones, we see genius. Because the people who are crazy enough to think they can change the world, are the ones who do.

Wow.

What made this commercial so powerful was that it wasn't BS, or a clever hook to get people to buy. Apple's Steve Jobs walked the talk himself. He was a relentless self-actualizer. In PBS's *One Last Thing* documentary, he laid out his vision of the world and his role in it (http://www.pbs.org/program/steve-jobs-one-last-thing/):

> When you grow up you tend to get told the world is the way it is and your life is just to live your life inside the world. Try not to bash into the walls too much. Try to have a nice family life, have fun, save a little money.
>
> That's a very limited life. Life can be much broader once

you discover one simple fact, and that is—everything around you that you call life, was made up by people that were no smarter than you. And you can change it, you can influence it, you can build your own things that other people can use.

The minute that you understand that you can poke life and actually something will, you know, if you push in, something will pop out the other side, that you can change it, you can mold it. That's maybe the most important thing. It's to shake off this erroneous notion that life is there and you're just gonna live in it, versus embrace it, change it, improve it, make your mark upon it.

I think that's very important and however you learn that, once you learn it, you'll want to change life and make it better, cause it's kind of messed up, in a lot of ways. Once you learn that, you'll never be the same again.

Wow again.

The reason I'm lathering on about Apple isn't because I'm an unabashed fan. OK, I am an unabashed fan. But apart from its technological whiz-bangery and Jobs's incredible personality, I think Apple nailed the second element critical to building a brand of the future (remember, the first element was discovering your own brand's essence). That second element is connecting on a higher, self-actualized level with your customer.

Simon Sinek did a terrific job explaining this esoteric concept in a TEDx talk (http://www.ted.com/talks/simon_sinek_how_great_leaders_inspire_action).

He began by saying Apple isn't the only company in their sector allowed to build new, cool things. It creates essentially the same products as other computer, phone, or tablet manufacturers. But there's a difference, something most of us can't verbalize.

That difference is that Apple understands its essence. And it connects with fans who share that essence.

Sinek summed up Apple's essence (he called it its "why"): "Everything we do, we believe in challenging the status quo. We believe in thinking differently." This essence manifests itself in everything Apple creates. And it builds a bond with consumers that goes beyond utility. If I, a humble writer, believe in challenging the status quo and thinking differently, I will find a kindred spirit in Apple. And once I understand that Apple "gets" me, I will find it much easier to buy products from Apple. These guys are like me, and I can trust them.

How deep does that connection go? Well, this book is being written on a MacBook Pro. For a fraction of the cost, I could've purchased a laptop from another manufacturer to work on. But I didn't. Go figure.

The beauty of connecting on the level of shared beliefs is that it liberates companies to innovate in areas where their competitors fear to tread. As Sinek described, you'd never buy an MP3 player from a computer company. But you'd buy one from Apple. I would venture that Apple could create a frying pan and we would line up the night before at the store to buy it. Knowing that Apple stands for challenging the status quo, we'd all accept that this frying pan would take our frying to new creative heights.

IT'S OK IF THEY DON'T LIKE YOU

In the last chapter I went through the Brand Compass process and how it can help map out what your brand stands for.

In this chapter, I highlighted the importance of connecting your brand's "why I exist" with the self-actualized consumer's "why I exist."

What I haven't explained is a process for figuring out *how* to align your brand's reason for existence with the consumer's.

I honestly don't think one exists.

Let me explain this on human terms. I meet you for the first time. I tell you what I like, what inspires me, and you do the same. Within a very short while, we can establish whether we'll be friends or not.

No process, no formula can artificially create this sort of chemistry. Truth is, humans haven't figured out a reliable methodology to ensure two people "click." Ask anyone who's used a dating service.

Sure, we can raise the odds that we'll like one another if we meet in a room of like-minded individuals. You fish, I fish, we're at a fishing convention. Yay. The only problem is, you think of fishing as blood sport, and I think of it as art in motion. Cue uncomfortable silence.

Of course, if I really want to "sell" myself to you, I can suppress my own personality, listen hard to your likes and dislikes, and mirror them. My story, values, priorities? Never mind.

If I do this, it won't take long for you to sniff out my insincerity. Think about the überfriendly guy at the picnic who ends up trying to sell you insurance. Best-case scenario, you never connect beyond a base, utilitarian level—yes, I need insurance, send me some literature, don't put me on the mailing list. Worst case, you avoid the guy like the plague and tell all your friends to do the same.

Big brands don't get this. Instead of digging deep into their own reason for existence and very selectively trying to make friends with consumers who aspire to the same ideals, they try to satisfy the lower-level needs of as many people as possible with an absolutely generic offering. They skip past the friendship and dating, treating consumers a bit like a one-night stand. Sure, it works sometimes. But it's no way to build a relationship, or a business.

Case in point—think of all the inane car ads you've seen come out of Detroit. Hip young couple jumps into boring car, drives around doing unbelievably fun, sexy things, winning the love and admiration of onlookers.

Now go and ask any hip young couple if this ad "sold" them on the car. Don't. Make. Me. Laugh. The ad may look like the company understands young couples, gets where they're coming from. But it's a completely superficial effort with the sincerity of, well, a car salesman.

Let's contrast that with Yvon Chouinard, and how he sold Patagonia's products right from the start. Chouinard loved the outdoors more than life itself, giving up creature comforts, money, food, and shelter just to climb, ski, and surf. He started making mountaineering gear out of necessity—all the products on the market sucked. His gear was great, because he knew how gear needed to look, feel and perform. Inevitably, his like-minded friends came to him for their gear. Then their friends came. And Patagonia was born.

Chouinard didn't try to get into the heads of the mass audience and position his product for the broadest possible appeal. He had a target audience of one—himself.

Chouinard behaved like an authentic human would. He made products consistent with his values and beliefs. If others had the same values, they'd buy the products and become friends. If they didn't, oh well.

So what's the lesson here? Keep Yvon Chouinard in mind as you develop your Brand Compass. Sweat bullets to make sure that compass absolutely reflects what you value and cherish as a human. And when you bring that brand to life, make sure it adheres to the compass with laser focus. Do this, and authenticity will radiate from your brand like a halo. Trust me—you'll find your audience. And they won't be fair-weather friends.

SANDING THE HOUSE, PAINTING THE HOUSE
This stuff is hard.

Digging into what your brand really is and who it's going to appeal to is weird and messy. And what do you get for your trouble? A bunch of words on a page. Great. Take that to the bank.

When I bring clients through this process, I often tell them the first part—the part we just went through—is like sanding a house, and the second like painting a house. The sanding is hard, knuckle-bruising work. It takes a long time, and at the end of it, what do you have to show? A house that's stripped down, not terribly attractive, and only halfway done. It's hard to see the big reward.

But if you sanded diligently, really put your back into it, the paint goes on beautifully, sticks like a charm, and the house looks like a million bucks for a long, long time. Do a crap job sanding, and the paint—even the glossiest paint—will blister and peel off before you know it. You'll have to go through the whole process again. *That's* discouraging.

So now we've gone through the sanding process, let's get onto the fun bit. How we bring this thing to life.

BUILD IT TO LAST

THE UNCOMFORTABLE EVOLUTION
OF THE SUSTAINABLE BRAND

I started my green ad agency in 2005, just before Al Gore's *Inconvenient Truth* turned every North American into a terrified, temporary environmentalist.

From the film's impact, you'd think Gore had invented sustainability. But it wasn't a new concept. Gro Brundtland defined the term in a UN report back in 1987 (http://conspect.nl/pdf/Our_Common_Future-Brundtland_Report_1987.pdf). Almost every generation in recent memory has had high-profile environmental champions, from Jacques Cousteau and Jane Goodall to Rachel Carson and Teddy Roosevelt. Long story short—sustainability has been knocking around our collective consciousness for quite some time.

Why then, hadn't it become ingrained in our culture the way consumption had?

My thinking was the two were always forced to appear in public as enemies, like wrestling archrivals. Why couldn't they put a tag team together and really kick butt?

OK, there were obvious reasons why.

For one, we collectively refused to see the need. The world seemed just fine. Besides, our job was consuming, and thinking about where our products came from or where they were going made our head hurt all the way to the mall.

This apathy was a godsend to companies. As mentioned earlier, they did their best to maintain the status quo by screaming like extras in a Godzilla movie about loss of competitiveness, crippling costs, and shareholder lynch mobs every time a special interest group made noises about greening production.

Understandably, this drove environmentalists nuts. Which also didn't help. Their frustrated demeanor made them look even more like a crazy fringe group.

So trying to get sustainability and consumption to work together was like counseling a couple with "irreconcilable differences." Ugly.

Gore's film, however, forced that couple to the therapist's office and made them start talking.

Mainstream consumers turned down their green signal jammers. We started to hear about companies making terrific products as sustainably as possible. There were even people out there buying these products, testing the waters for us. Conscious consumers, cultural creatives, the LOHAS set, pick your moniker.

It was a relatively small audience—despite all the breathlessly optimistic "given a choice, people will buy green" research. And they weren't always mavens who'd inspire others to follow suit—quite the opposite. Many rubbed people the wrong way. They were wealthy movie stars, narcissistic Eat Pray Lovers, or smugly sincere college students.

This was about the time I rolled up my sleeves and got involved.

I came on the scene in typical ad guy fashion, assuming that taking sustainability into the mainstream was as simple as making it sexy. Heck, I'd made antacid and denture cream sexy. How hard could this be?

Very hard, it turns out.

The first eight-hundred-pound gorilla I ran into was greenwashing.

Greenwashing means making green claims that are overstated or untrue. But wait. Overstating or amplifying minor product attributes is a pillar of advertising. Now it was a bad thing?

Turns out consumers had a bit of a double standard for green and non-green claims. If I told you my perfume would make you irresistible and it didn't, you'd forgive my puffery. But if I promised my brand was saving the rainforest and it didn't, you'd gather the villagers, grab the pitchforks, and hunt me down.

Greenwashing was just the tip of the iceberg. There were plenty of other unfamiliar problems to deal with. Complex claims that didn't lend themselves to ad sound bites. A dizzying array of confusing green certification programs. A lack of universal metrics that made comparative claims impossible. New issues popping up like a Whack-a-Mole game. And the "what do we do that consumers will appreciate?" conundrum.

I could dig into each of these at length. But that would take us down a very long, deep rabbit hole. Instead, let me leave it at "greening brands was hard."

It was also, however, necessary. Traditional means of production were being exposed daily as harmful to the planet or overly reliant on cheap, plentiful fossil fuels. Governments were gearing up legislation to start punishing polluters. Employees—especially young job seekers—were looking for companies that had a strong stance on sustainability. And companies like GE, Ford, and Wal-Mart were showing with their full-forward march into green that getting in the game wasn't optional.

Much water has passed under the bridge since then, and many case studies written. But don't be fooled—it's still the Wild West.

I find this exciting—we're the ones who get to develop green marketing tools that become the formulas of the future. In the meantime, it pays to reflect on how other brands have succeeded.

SEVENTH GENERATION VS. METHOD VS. REPLENISH VS. GREEN WORKS

From a marketer's perspective, a great place to look for lessons branding sustainability is in the cleaner aisle.

It's a relatively simple, straightforward category. Before the rise of green, cleaners were commodity purchases. People just wanted something they could trust to get the job done. Naturally, that efficacy demanded harsh ingredients.

As sustainability became an issue, people adjusted their definition of "trust." They wanted cleaners they could trust would clean but also trust not to harm their families.

Looking at the players in the green cleaner aisle is instructive. There are some very unique brands out there, with very unique marketing approaches.

Let's start with one of the originals.

Seventh Generation was founded in 1988 by entrepreneurs with a strong commitment to sustainability. Right down to its name—a reference to the Great Law of the Iroquois (http://www.indigenous-people.net/iroqcon.htm), "In our every deliberation, we must consider the impact of our decisions on the next seven generations"—the brand exudes a sense of meaning beyond cleaning.

Since they've appeared on my grocery shelves, Seventh Generation bottles have been a generic white, giving me the impression that making the product beautiful was not a top priority. True, they stood out in a sea of slickly marketed mainstream brands. But they gave off so many hippie cues that I invariably questioned if they worked as well as they preached.

But what do I know? The company has stood the test of time. It's seen healthy, although by no means meteoric, growth. The product line is expanding, and the commitment to greater good is undimmed. Not only that, but Seventh Generation has blazed trails in the category, becoming the first homecare company to voluntarily disclose ingredients on the label, the first company with a fully compostable outer shell package, and the first consumer products company with the USDA-Certified Biobased label, to name just a few accolades. No slouches here.

Seventh Generation understands its higher purpose, and where that purpose intersects with the higher-order needs of a very specific conscious consumer group. One could argue the brand single-handedly grew the market for other green cleaners, all while demonstrating unassailable credibility.

Lesson: Integrity and authenticity do work as marketing differentiators. But if you're going to lead with purpose, be prepared to bypass the vast majority of mainstream consumers who still need to know effective cleaning is priority one.

Now, to paraphrase Monty Python, for something completely different: Method.

I still remember the day my wife came home with her first bottle of Method dish soap. Actually, I wasn't sure it was soap—the bottle looked like a frosted hourglass made of squishy silicon. I thought it might be a newfangled stress ball or table lamp.

She put it proudly on the counter next to the sink, then squeezed out a neon stream of cleaning liquid. Both of us felt as though we'd suddenly become cooler people.

Cool defines Method. Yes, the company has the same sort of sustainability priorities as Seventh Generation, but that's where the similarity ends.

That squishy hourglass soap dispenser was designed by Karim Rashid. As far as I know, it's the only cleaner bottle created by a designer so famous he can go by his first name without getting laughed at.

Cool also features prominently in Method's website and advertising. For the longest time (long being a relative term—Method was started in 2001) the company's messaging featured naked people cleaning to underline its commitment to nontoxic, naturally derived ingredients.

The logo looks MoMA. The founders were feted by PETA. And products like its eight-times-concentrated laundry detergent define innovation in the category.

I love Method and its playful, irreverent, innovative approach to sustainability. Turns out I'm not the only one. In 2006, just five years after launch, the company was named the seventh fastest growing private company in America by Fast Company. And in 2012, Method joined forces with Ecover, creating the world's largest green cleaner company.

So what's the lesson here? First, give people fun, good-looking stuff that works, and they'll give you their dollar. Duh. Second, use sustainability as an innovation filter to come up with cooler products, but use it sparingly as a marketing tool if you want the attention of mainstream consumers.

Now, let's talk about Replenish.

This is a company near and dear to my heart. First, because I've known its founder Jason Foster since launch. And second, because Jason gives fantastic sound bites.

I still remember the day Jason sat on a panel at the Sustainable Brands conference and told us that big companies were innovation dinosaurs because their vested interests demanded protecting out-of-touch cash cows.

He was sitting next to a panelist from Unilever at the time. It was a lively discussion, to say the least.

Jason has backed his audacious claims with an innovative product. Replenish is a modular cleaner. The upper portion of the bottle, crafted in beautiful heavy-duty plastic (with a nod to Method's design sensibility), is empty. No cleaner at all. The bottom piece, which snaps on, is a pod holding concentrated cleaning "juice." With a squeeze, the pod dispenses concentrate into a mixing cup inside the empty bottle. Add water and, hey presto, you have a bottle of cleaner. When the pod is empty, you recycle it and buy another.

Where Method's design was a cool idea, Replenish's design is a sustainability groundbreaker. It eliminates water, which comprises the bulk of any cleaner's shipping weight. It cuts down the amount of plastic you throw in the recycling bin, from an entire bottle down to a small replacement pod. And it puts forward a credible money-saving-through-conservation argument, equating old-fashioned throw-away bottles with money thrown out the window.

Lesson: There's something to be said for starting with a blank slate. Replenish's ethos is interwoven with its product design. It's all about shaking up the status quo as you shake the water/concentrate mix.

Rounding out our selection is Clorox Green Works. This is the only product in the bunch that was born from a big brand. While it may not be as innovative as Replenish, it's proof that being big doesn't doom you to being an innovation dinosaur. In fact, size comes with advantages.

When big brands began to sense rising consumer awareness of sustainability in the early 2000s, they knew they had to innovate or become the dinosaurs Foster described. Green credentials needed to be burnished quickly, and in-house teams weren't bringing it.

That led to a raft of acquisitions. Unilever bought Ben & Jerry's, Danone bought Stonyfield Farms, Clorox bought Burt's Bees, to name just a few. Each time, the purchase was greeted with derision in the green business community. In most cases, the marriages disproved the critics. For Clorox, the partnership with Burt's helped the behemoth accelerate up the green learning curve, leading to a more sustainable supply chain and greatly reduced waste to landfill. Surprising as it may sound, the benefits went both ways. Clorox actually helped Burt's create a more virtuous product—thanks to the giant's technology, the average Burt's product went from 97 percent to 99 percent natural (http://www.theguardian.com/sustainable-business/burts-bees-clorox-sustainable-change).

It was one thing to buy a green company. But when Clorox created Green Works cleaners on its own, the cries of derision sounded once more. Heck, this was a company whose *name* was synonymous with nasty chemicals. Surely this was just a cynical greenwash doomed to failure.

Not so.

Clorox did a bunch of things right. While most of the ingredients were less environmentally harmful, some of the stuff in the bottle wasn't squeaky green. But *all* the ingredients—good and bad—were listed on the label, opening the kimono of transparency wider than it ever had been before.

There were two other important bits on the label. First, the Clorox logo. Conscious consumers may have held their noses at the mere mention of the name, but mainstream folks trusted the brand. Seeing Clorox meant this green cleaner actually *cleaned*. A coup in a category that equated sustainability with loss of efficacy.

Second, the label featured an endorsement from the Sierra Club. Yes, the Sierra Club and Clorox on the same label. Definitely a first, and a very effective means of establishing legitimacy in a market tainted by greenwash.

Clorox backed the new product with massive advertising dollars and prime shelf space. A year after launch, Green Works owned 20 percent of the green cleaner market.

So what's the lesson from Green Works? There's more than one shade of green. While conscious consumers may not have bought the product, the light-green mainstream did. Building sustainability into your brand and targeting it effectively will help you get a piece of a pie that's only increasing in size.

THE GREATEST (NEVER-ENDING) DIFFERENTIATOR

Sustainability is key to building a futureproof brand. It puts you on the right side of environmental legislation. It helps ensure the employees in your company—your brand's best sales team—are happy and motivated by more than money. It keeps production efficient and somewhat insulated from the vagaries of rising fossil fuel prices, which helps maintain competitive pricing.

There's one other very big reason why sustainability is important. We're never going to get it 100 percent right, which means there will always be room for improvement. That, in turn, will provide endless inspiration for innovation. And those innovations, positioned properly, will become effective differentiators.

Think Nike Air. Think Intel Inside. Think iTunes. What green innovations will claim a place alongside them?

WHAT'S NEXT?

INNOVATION, A MOST-USED, ABUSED WORD

My generation has experienced some pretty breathtaking product innovations. The personal computer, mobile phone, digital audio, the Internet—none of them existed when I was born.

Despite that, my time in mainstream advertising went by relatively undisturbed by innovation upheavals. Game changers were few and far between. What we were generally given to sell were tweaks on existing products. Same car, new chrome. Same pop, new can.

That meant we could get good at positioning an improvement to our audience, figure out what hooks worked, and go home for the weekend feeling we were ahead of the Stupid Curve.

That's all over now.

Thanks to rapidly evolving tech, drastically reduced prototyping costs, incredible tools for sharing ideas, and a shift from big corporatism to small entrepreneurialism (to name just a few factors), we're seeing innovation become the new marketing. Great products, not great ideas for selling products, are winning the day. When Steve Jobs was luring Pepsi executive John Sculley to Apple, he summed it up nicely: "Do you want to sell sugar water for the rest of your life, or do you want to come with me and change the world?" (http://www.bloomberg.com/video/66625228-bloomberg-game-changers-steve-jobs.html).

Not surprisingly, it's easier to talk about innovation than do it. If you want to bring big ideas to life, you need to be willing to uproot the status quo, take risks, and fail—things shareholders don't smile upon. So most big companies choose to cautiously evolve cash cow brands and spend heavily on advertising to point out each miniscule improvement. The scenario Yves Behar described when he said, "Advertising is the price companies pay for being unoriginal" still carries the day (http://icetothebrim.com/2009/advertising-is-the-price-companies-pay-for-being-unoriginal/).

This inability to create meaningful change has led to upheaval from outside. While big brand executives tinker, garage entrepreneurs invent bullets that will take those brands out of commission. Music industry, meet Napster.

I have nothing against this sort of business Darwinism. The music industry was due for a revolution. Many slow-moving bureaucratic companies are. However, constantly usurping the establishment comes with a price. Expertise and learning is lost, supply chains need to be reassembled, efficiencies rediscovered. All the little things that made the big brand successful for so long, all the things that took the big company years to assemble and tweak, all these things have to be pieced together again like a puzzle. While slow and steady definitely don't win the race, there's no reason for the hares to kill all the turtles.

There is another way. Big brands need to look at points where their innovation process logjams and start innovating *there*. Whether it's A.G. Lafley decreeing that Procter would look outside for new ideas instead of keeping innovation in-house, IBM using its network technology to create Global Idea Jams, or Clorox acquiring Burt's

Bees to jump-start its sustainability program.

Marketing used to sit at the head of the table, a place that innovation now fills. I don't see that changing anytime soon. As our world becomes a global village, the new universal language will be innovation. All of us will speak it at a healthy clip. It's a language less adaptive brands will have to learn, if they hope to survive and thrive.

Here's what they're going to have to learn right out of the gate.

OUTSIDE-THE-JAR THINKING

Mike Maddock is a friend and mentor. His innovation firm, Maddock Douglas, also bought my green brand agency and brought me aboard as head of green innovation.

Speaking with Mike is like a breath of fresh air—uncomplicated, commonsense, and full of "Why didn't I think of that" epiphanies.

One of the first things Mike impressed on me was that companies lose the ability to innovate because their teams lose the ability to see the world clearly. He called it inside-the-jar thinking.

"When you join a company, you see with great clarity things that could be improved—for about six months," says Mike. "After that, you've been indoctrinated with all the reasons why those improvements just can't be made. 'We tried it before,' or 'The boss would hate it.' Although the world still looks the same, you're looking at it from the company's constrained, inside-the-jar perspective."

To fight inside-the-jar thinking, big companies often bring aboard consultants like myself for projects. They're fun engagements. I love watching the company team emerging from their psychological jars, sniffing the fresh air, and really ideating with gusto.

The problem is, few companies see the process through. More often than not, the great ideas are put down on paper, the consultant paid, and...nothing. The company team members slip back into their jars, and a million reasons for holding off on implementation are brought forward.

I have, however, found a way to keep the innovation flowing, even in the absence of corporate willpower. I call it the idea slush fund.

I created an idea slush fund of sorts as a creative director. In actual fact, it was more of an unspoken agreement between my clients and my teams. We had an understanding we would produce work in complete compliance with their wishes—98 percent of the time. In return, they would humor us by indulging our crazy ideas for communication 2 percent of the time. Some terrific work came out of that 2 percent. Once it was produced, clients actually loved some of it, so it went "live" and built their brands. A few pieces we created got picked up in other markets, where our clients' compatriots lauded them for creating such visionary stuff.

One of the better-known incarnations of the slush fund concept is Google's "20% program" (http://www.wired.com/2013/08/20-percent-time-will-never-die/), where employees are allowed to pursue passion projects aligned with company business one day a week, or 20 percent of the time. Ironically, this much-lauded program is still an ad hoc affair. There's no handbook or official process. Just encouragement for bringing fresh, outside-the-jar thinking to the business, with the possibility of implementation held out as a carrot.

THE INNOVATION PIPELINE

Looking at the company from outside the jar is critical for spotting weaknesses and opportunities. But somewhere along the line, you have to start innovating.

This can be a daunting task, especially if there's no fence to focus your thinking. The innovation pipeline is a tool that answers this call.

I have Mike Maddock to thank for introducing it to me—Maddock Douglas has hammered out a powerful pipeline methodology—but innovators of every stripe have their own versions.

In essence, the pipeline forces us to think of great ideas that will keep the brand fresh not just in the next quarter but five years down the road, ten years down the road, to infinity and beyond.

Ironically, the trick in this is not to think in terms of time, but strategy. It's about mapping out the world your brand inhabits, the world its consumers inhabit, the world we all inhabit, and charting a likely course that will keep you on trend, in people's minds, and a step ahead of the competition.

To make that easier, Maddock's pipeline is divided into three increments of innovation, each addressing specific strategic challenges along the brand's life cycle.

Evolutionary Innovation

If your brand is doing well, or perhaps losing a bit of its glow, there's no need for an overhaul. Staying fresh might simply involve the odd touch-up over the next one to three years. Radical change would be counterproductive, alienating the people who have already discovered your brand, who love it, and who are telling their friends about it. It ain't broke. Don't fix it.

So what do evolutionary innovations look like? Tweaks to design, enhanced user experience, better service support, partnerships, line extensions, anything that doesn't alter the fundamental bits consumers love while enhancing things that will surprise and delight them.

Evolutionary innovations should dominate your pipeline and your innovation budget, especially when it comes to the short term. They're going to be the lifeblood of your brand, keeping it competitive in the pauses between your great leaps forward.

Since the death of Steve Jobs, Apple has lived in this space (for better or worse). Phones have gotten thinner, tablets have better displays, there are fun new colors to choose from. And the stock price continues to soar.

Differentiating Innovation

My use of Apple as an example of evolutionary innovation wasn't coincidental. Apple today is coasting nicely on small improvements. But this isn't enough from a brand that has taught consumers to expect big ideas at regular intervals. Already, people are starting to question if Apple has lost its mojo. The brand needs some difficult but necessary innovations to differentiate itself.

Had Steve Jobs lived, the next breakthrough might have been in education reform, an area he felt needed drastic overhaul. This would've been a textbook case of differentiating innovation, Apple-style.

Core to the Apple brand is a promise to consumers that the tech giant will regularly transform moribund categories, bring them into the future, and make them exciting and fun once again—just what iPad did for reading, or iPod and iTunes did for music. This isn't easy stuff. It takes years to execute. But in Apple's case, it's critical if you want to keep your believers believing.

Differentiating innovations are difficult and costly, but they're necessary to ensure the brand's viability into the future. In my eyes, Toyota's hybrid drive system provides a great example, as does GE's Ecomagination. Both have redefined their category, left competitors scrambling to catch up, and given consumers entirely new reasons to love the brands.

In the pipeline, differentiating innovations should be prioritized behind evolutionary innovation. They are important but not quite as pressing. They are ideas that will, if properly developed, come online in five to ten years.

Revolutionary Innovation

Many garage entrepreneurs (at least the ones we read about) start with revolutionary ideas. These are the monster innovations that explode out of nowhere, get the headlines, and annihilate the competition.

Revolutionary innovations usually change more than their categories. The invention of snowboards, for example, changed the entire image of winter sport, produced Olympians and movie stars, spawned new clothing industries, even brought new style and excitement to its competitor, skiing.

Understandably, ideas like this don't come along every day. Many successful brands may never generate a revolutionary idea on their own. However, every brand that understands its reason to exist and its consumers' higher-level needs can develop a nose and passion for revolutionary ideas. It's less about invention and more about combining existing technologies in new ways to satisfy needs that consumers feel, but may have trouble expressing. When you think of Henry Ford's Model T and production line, there was no terribly new technology at work. He simply saw a nascent need (make cars affordable to the masses) and a new way to do it (break down the assembly along a moving line). Ford's famous quote—"If I had asked people what they wanted, they would have said faster horses"—also underlines what made this idea revolutionary. The audience wanted cheap cars but couldn't express that need using their existing frames of reference. Thus, when Model T's started rolling off the production lines, people were as much amazed as grateful. It was as if someone had read their minds.

Sitting down to brainstorm revolutionary ideas is useful, even if you only devote a fraction of the time and budget to it that you do evolutionary and differentiating innovations. That's because revolutionary innovations are manifestations of your brand's North Star—they're "real" expressions of your brand's mission and purpose. Saying, "One day, this brand will be able to (insert revolutionary idea)" is a wonderful way of aligning your team and letting them know which stars you actually want to shoot for.

THE JOY OF FAILURE

One of the most important elements of innovation is the understanding that nobody gets it right the first time, every time, or even most of the time. The best we can hope for is to create a broad strokes idea that gets everybody nodding, then turn to fast fail innovation to fill in the rest.

The essence of fast fail is trying out lots of ideas, quickly and cheaply. Prototypes can be duct tape and cardboard. Tweaks can be made with scissors and felt pens. The point is to keep an open mind, high level of enthusiasm, and large pool of test subjects happy to tell you what works and, more important, what doesn't.

Fast fail works when enthusiasm for a better end product overrides territoriality or ego. People who can't stand to see their ideas get stomped don't do well with fast fail. Personally, I've always been a big fan, having had enough ideas in my time to know that every crushed innovation spawns five other good ones. Anyone who thinks their idea can't be improved on shouldn't be in the idea game.

If we're talking about brands that want to make themselves more resilient and futureproof, fast fail is indispensible. It's one big feedback loop that allows you to constantly trim your brand's rudder and avoid big diversions in the wrong direction. There simply is no better way to connect with your consumer than to let them codesign your innovation so that it truly works for them.

IS IT BEAUTIFUL?

THE PHEROMONES OF DESIGN

I'm not a designer. And that, from my perspective, is highly unfair.

I've always loved how design looked and how it worked. I tried to add a design sensibility to my own life, doing things in ways that not only made common sense but created beauty. Unfortunately, my talent didn't match my aspirations.

In high school, for example, I dreamed of pin-striping and airbrushing hot rods for a living. Unfortunately, I couldn't trace a straight line and I drew like Napoleon Dynamite. In college, I tried to make money as a photographer. Once more, that lack-of-talent thing got in the way. I'll stop at these two anecdotes, but I can assure you it's been a recurring theme in my life.

So imagine my delight when I went into advertising and was partnered with an art director. A guy who could draw, shoot striking photos, lay a million elements out in a print ad and make them look beautiful and natural, all while slouched in his seat with feet up on his desk. I was in heaven by association.

Happily, I've kept talented designers close at hand ever since.

I'm not alone in my passion for design. I'd go out on a limb and say we all appreciate it. The problem is, few of us can express why.

That's because good design elicits an intuitive response. A gut reaction. It attracts us without a word, like pheromones. Powerful stuff.

Ironically, design gets short shrift in business for precisely this reason. It's hard to quantify the intuitive with charts and spreadsheets. Consequently, design gets pushed to the back of the priority list, way behind stuff bean counters can wrap their heads around, like engineering.

What's more, because it makes complicated things appear effortless, most of us believe design *is* effortless. Every client can do it, and the spouse of every client can do it better. It isn't surprising that designers face incredulity when they slide their rate sheets across the table.

Design hasn't done itself any favors. Technology gave every Mac monkey the tools to do reasonable design, with less talent than I had as a hot rod painter. Combine that with crowdsourcing design services, and you suddenly have self-respecting designers competing with guys in the basement for $300 logo and graphics jobs. It's a race for the bottom.

I'm here to put a well-designed stake in the ground. If your brand wants to exist in a turbulent world, design is your new best friend. And not the $300 crowdsourced variety of design. I'm talking pheromone-emitting stuff that attracts everyone with eyes.

IT'S NOT HOW IT LOOKS—IT'S HOW IT WORKS

Design has gotten a bad rap for coming across as "pretty", elitist, and frivolous. Dressing up a three to look like a nine. People who think about design this way, as expendable window dressing, are missing the point.

Steve Jobs nailed it when he said the thing about design isn't that it looks great, but that it works great. He isn't talking about design working to attract consumers, either, like a fishing lure. He's talking about how design actually improves how products work. Making them do what they do better.

This has traditionally been an engineer's domain. The problem is, engineers don't think like designers. Engineers understand technology and think in terms of making technology work as well as possible.

A great example of products created by engineers are VCR remote controls from the 1980s. As technology increased the computing power of the chips in each remote handset, they became capable of executing far more functions. Thinking it was a shame not to tap all those goodies, the engineers built units that packed scores of features into each remote. The user interface (in simple English, the buttons) shrank and shrank. The instruction manuals grew and grew.

As a teen, I worked in my Dad's TV store, selling things like VCRs. I saw the human effect of this movement. *Absolute disaster* would be the words that come to mind. In eight years on the job, I don't think I managed to teach a single customer how to prerecord a show or record a show at the same time every week. Most customers never got past Stop, Play, Rewind. That old joke about people not knowing how to program the clock on their VCR? No joke.

In contrast, a designer thinks in human terms first. If designers had been the ones challenged to create better remotes for VCRs in the 1980s, I'm certain the handsets would have looked different.

Where engineers began by exploring what the technology could do, designers would begin by exploring what the average person could do. Or, even better, what the average person could do without instruction.

You can see how these divergent approaches would yield vastly different outcomes. I'd wager that VCR remotes, had they been designed by designers back in the 1980s, might have looked more like iPods. And everyone's grandma would've known how to record the same show at the same time every week, not to mention how to program the clock in seconds flat.

This anecdote cuts to the core of why design is needed today more than ever. Earlier in the book, I described the technological maelstrom most consumers find themselves in. They are inundated with technology that seems to be designed more for zealots than casual users. They're constantly behind the Stupid Curve, trying to figure out the exponentially growing number of tech tools they're expected to master, all with their own unique, quirky operating system.

Like the bat signal, I think we all need to send up a beacon pleading the designers of the world to save us from our self-induced technological chaos.

Of course we can't do that. But you can. A brand that wants to win over consumers today, and in the future, will make simple, human-centric design a big priority. Do it, before your competitors do.

THE PSYCHOLOGY OF SIMPLE

Arguably the first casualty of technological overload is our attention span. The more we speed up, the less we are able to absorb or reflect. This makes us not only lousy strategic thinkers and decision makers but lousy humans, as well (http://www.gdrc.org/icts/i-overload/infoload.html).

The technological impetus to accelerate makes us impatient with ourselves and others. We become easily frustrated by obstacles, like infants trying to fit round pegs into square holes. Our sense of wonder, peace, and reflection are kicked to the curb by never-ending pings.

We could spend hours debating the sanity of this state of affairs, but for the moment let's just say humans need a helping hand. Something to calm our jangled nerves, mow down obstructions, and perhaps even give us opportunity to pause a moment and smile.

That's what design does.

Good design makes complicated things simple. Great design does it while inspiring us. Think of the first time you spun an iPod thumb wheel and realized you wouldn't need instructions to figure this thing out. Or the first time you looked at a Prius's mileage screen and understood how easing off the gas at green lights would boost your mileage—again, without instructions. These experiences stop us in our tracks with the realization there are smart people out there using their powers for good.

A short while ago, I had the good fortune to stroll through LA's new international airport terminal. In my humble opinion, this place takes the design cake. Airports are generally anxious places, full of people pretending to be busy on their phones and tablets, their daily dose of tech irritation amplified by the frustrations that come with air travel. But in LA, I didn't see fast-walking, anxious people. Instead, I saw many of us (my family included) looking up at the incredible design pieces and art—3-D projected clocks and glockenspiels, massive virtual lutes you could pluck as you walked by to create your own music, countless little visual wonders that reminded us we were in the city of dreams. We put away the phones, sat back, and smiled, even slowed down to play a bit. Heck, the check-in counter could wait.

I believe design's power to simplify and humanize can do more than buffer the intimidation of technology. It also presents a common language for our hyperconnected global village. With language comes communication, understanding, and shared experiences—the building blocks of a common culture.

Think about your last trip to a foreign country where you didn't speak the language. How did you ask for the bathroom or convey what you wanted on the menu? Most likely with a bit of amateur mime.

Not only did you get what you wanted (well, most of the time) but you probably also raised a smile with your hosts. Where there had been mild mistrust and tension, there was now the flickering of shared humanity, a bond.

Design is mime. It conveys meaning without words. As such, it can also create a bond in situations where lack of lingua franca creates barriers.

It can also create a common language between people who share the same language. On a number of tech projects, I was brought in to translate nerd into English. On sustainability marketing projects, I was brought in to translate hippie into business. Either way, I ended up augmenting written words with iconography and symbols—a language understood by everyone, a language easy to embrace.

My former boss at Palmer Jarvis, Chris Staples, was a big advocate of ads that worked without words. His thinking was that we lived in a postliterate society, where writing inhibited uptake, created frustration, and led to rejection of the message. Instead of creating warm feelings around our clients' products, language led to frustration and switching off.

Nathaniel Hawthorne famously said easy reading is damn hard writing. I'd argue from experience that the easiest form of reading, design, makes for the hardest work of all. But the psychological rewards make it a top priority for brands trying to futureproof themselves.

PHASE ZERO

So how do you create this sort of design? The timeless, simple, and inspiring stuff that everyone covets and so few achieve?

I thought it might be helpful to get a practitioner's perspective, so I enlisted Mark Busse—Mark runs his own design firm, teaches the subject at the college level, organizes design education events, and has just been named a fellow of the Graphic Designers of Canada (or GDC)—he's one of the youngest practitioners ever to receive this honor. Mark is a one-man force of nature on the subject of good versus bad design. And he's always happy to lend a sound bite.

Mark didn't waste any time with niceties, digging right into a chronic problem that continues to stand in the way of great design: lack of strategic thinking.

"Too many clients still pigeonhole design as window dressing, not a tool for building business. I'm amazed how many people walk in our door convinced they need, say, a new logo and name. They have no data confirming the old logo and name aren't working. It's just their hunch. Can you imagine ordering a fleet of new delivery trucks on a hunch? Wouldn't happen."

To rectify this state of affairs, Busse introduced what he calls Phase Zero. In essence, it's the step that happens before the first step in successful design. "If we're going to create design that builds the client's business, we first need to establish what the real problem is. That's Phase Zero."

Busse says Phase Zero challenges preconceptions the moment it's tabled. It makes clients reconsider the depth of their own strategic thinking. It exposes ambiguities and generalities in the brief. And it forces a reexamination of the design budget. "To us, starting without Phase Zero is like having a client say they want us to build a car—period. Who the hell knows how much a car costs without knowing what *kind* of car and features you need?"

Another Phase Zero shocker is that it comes with a money-back guarantee. Busse gets clients to carve off a small chunk of their budget for Phase Zero, and he returns the money if they discover the real problem can't be solved with design. The way Busse sees it, he wants to work on projects where his team's efforts have a viable chance of creating success.

So how does Phase Zero work? First, it digs into the brand's higher purpose, the consumer's higher-order need, and where the two intersect—the same elements I underline as critical to building a futureproof brand. As Busse says, "We need to know what the brand stands for, how it walks and talks, whom it appeals to and why. We need data; we need facts. Only by doing this heavy lifting up front can we actually get insight into where misalignment is happening, where the brand is missing the mark. That misalignment becomes the insight that we craft our brief around."

Phase Zero does more than lay the groundwork for a project—it shifts client thinking. "When clients see how much auditing, how much data, how much analysis goes into Phase Zero, they begin to appreciate that good design is based on more than aesthetics and can do more than spruce up letterhead."

Phase Zero's emphasis on data sets the tone for every other step of Busse's projects. He's a big believer in measurement and quantification, a concept that seems antithetical to many design clients. "Design feels subjective, full of decisions based on 'like–not like' criteria. To elevate its value among business decision makers, we need to introduce objective criteria and ways of measuring if it's actually doing the job."

Phase Zero, like the rest of Busse's process, involves hard, messy work that demands client participation. But he thinks the finished product is worth the slog. "Design creates a powerful impression of a brand— if you don't get it right, it's a powerful negative impression. This is a big deal. We need to have our clients pouring their heart into the process to guarantee the end product is something they can cheer for."

There's been much ado about the democratization of design in the past few years. Designers of all stripes are logging on to design "clearinghouse" websites and competing for quickie projects with miniscule budgets. If Phase Zero was designed to elevate design as a business tool, the move to online quick and cheap design is turning the profession into a commodity and pushing designers into the same order-taker box as your local print shop.

"Trust is critical to this process. You have to work hard to get at the essence of your brand, to help your designer shape it, and to deliver it in the best way possible. You have to trust your designer when it comes to making hard choices about what works best in a tiebreaker situation. That simply doesn't happen when you contract with a designer online for three hundred dollars."

Again and again, Busse underlined the importance of authenticity in design. He believed the difference between good and great designers came down to an ability to tap into the intangible human qualities of a brand. And a successful project depended on clients understanding, and being able to convey, connection points with consumers that transcended superficial marketing clichés.

Much more than meets the eye, *n'est-ce pas*?

HAVE THE CONVERSATION

SECRECY IS DEAD—DON'T WORRY ABOUT IT

One hot topic of conversation in my circles is the insane online sharing our kids engage in.

The chatter tends to focus on horror stories, usually involving a teen's less-than-intelligent use of their smartphone camera.

Parental outrage isn't a big deal. Kids have been shocking their parents since Cain and Abel. But a sea change is happening here, and hypersharing teenagers are just the tip of the iceberg.

For example, there's been a move to brazen sharing of state secrets, headlined by Julian Assange and Edward Snowden. While the motives, methods, and mental health of these two gentlemen can be debated, there's no denying their actions helped crystallize public antipathy toward the opaque, clandestine nature of government.

In my own profession, the magic of secrets has been replaced by the nobility of sharing all. Back in the 1970s, McDonald's made a huge deal of its Big Mac special sauce, keeping the ingredients a closely guarded secret to enhance the product's uniqueness and desirability.

Today, McDonald's Canada has created a successful ad campaign giving consumers the straight, unvarnished truth about its food. Heck, there are even videos explaining how to make the secret sauce with ingredients you can find in any supermarket (http://www.dailymail.co.uk/news/article-2171302/How-make-Big-Mac-home-McDonalds-chef-explains-secret.html). The fast-food giant's reasons for coming clean are easy to understand—films like *Super Size Me* positioned McDonald's as a keeper of secrets that were making us fat and ill. But if you consider the success of McDonald's Truth campaign, you get the sense sharing is becoming the new Unique Selling Proposition. Brands that tell all are rewarded. Even if the food still makes us fat and ill.

On another note, Elon Musk of Tesla has just thrown open a raft of his company's patents for competitors to learn from and copy (http://blogs.hbr.org/2014/07/elon-musks-patent-decision-reflects-three-strategic-truths/). There are a number of possible reasons why Musk is letting the competition crib from his innovation sheet—for example, expanding the electric car category more rapidly or cementing Tesla's role as a supplier of innovations that competitors can't replicate—but it was the reaction from shareholders that was noteworthy. Far from reading Musk the riot act, they pushed share prices up 10 percent (http://qz.com/222006/elon-musks-radical-patent-strategy-for-tesla-is-already-paying-off/#/). Shareholders love sharing, too, it seems.

I believe climate change has been a catalyst in the sharing movement, as has globalization. But at the root of it all is our newfound technological prowess. We're able to put information out into the world and dig up secrets at an unprecedented pace. We've become insatiable in our lust for inside information, with breathless admiration for brands that tell all, and technology that keeps opening the kimono wider and wider.

You might think this sounds like a scary, unstable state of affairs. I would agree. That's beside the point. Instead of worrying how hypersharing could bite our brand in the bum, let's focus instead on how it can help us accelerate our insight gathering, our innovation, and our capacity to communicate.

SOCIAL DOESN'T EQUAL TECHNOLOGY

In most of my conversations with brand stewards, the subject of social media comes up. Invariably they tell me they have their bases covered, and rattle off all the tools they use—Facebook, LinkedIn, Twitter, YouTube—you name it, they got it. When I ask what they're using them for, the conversation grinds to a halt.

Technology isn't social. Apps aren't social. "Like" buttons aren't social.

Communicating—and here I put the emphasis on listening, not speaking—is social. In fact, I'd say monologuing out your product news and ad messages is decidedly antisocial.

We have, however, become a quick-fix culture, and social media gadgetry plays to the worst of these tendencies. We'll install share buttons on each of our online press releases, then wonder why everyone doesn't pass them along. Must be a bug in the program.

When I talk about social media in my speeches, I use a very low-tech visual to illustrate the ideal scenario. It's an antique photo of two ladies gossiping over the backyard fence while hanging out the wash. It may look like an impossibly slow way to share news and views, but if you've lived in a small town, you'll understand "over the fence" information spreads like wildfire.

I know from experience. Back in my student days, I lived in a Swiss village, doing a marketing internship at a watch company. Nobody in the village spoke English, and I didn't speak French. I didn't interact socially with anyone outside the company for at least three weeks. But on my first day off, I strolled down the main street into the butcher shop. My entrance killed the lively chitchat in the store, as everyone stopped to stare. As I left, the conversation resumed. I could decipher enough words to know they were sharing the highlights of my bio with each other. It was like they'd read my résumé.

We humans are social animals. Give us a question worth answering, and we'll gladly answer it. Provide us with news worth spreading, and we'll happily spread it. Money isn't a motive here—we like to feel connected, respected, and somehow valued for our thoughts and opinions.

So how do you use this information to build a brand that is relevant today and tomorrow? I believe there are three specific areas where well-developed social skills can provide a leg up. You can ask people for ideas, ask them how to make your ideas better, and ask them to tell their friends about your ideas.

Of course, before you do that, you have to find the right people to talk to.

FIND YOUR FRIENDS

A few years back, I set out to publish at least one blog every two weeks. These blogs were designed to cement my reputation as a thought leader. I wanted to be the futureproof brand go-to guy.

The blogs started to flow. They were published in high-profile journals like *Fast Company* and *Huffington Post*, then sent to more specialized sites like *GreenBiz*, *Sustainable Brands*, and *TreeHugger*. I fired them out to LinkedIn groups, tweeted about them, signed off my e-mails with the latest story. Everything linked back to my website. My posse of followers started to grow. Conversations happened. Web visits went through the roof.

The number of new clients I acquired through these efforts? Zero. Every piece of new business I got came from tried-and-true methods—networking, public speaking, dialing up old friends in new jobs.

When people asked how the blogging was going (aka was it working?), I back rationalized, saying no new clients had signed up because of my writing but most prospects had checked me out online before hiring me. My blogging provided some sort of reassurance that I was indeed the man for the job.

I didn't know if any of my new clients *had* checked out my thought leadership pieces prior to signing on the dotted line. It was just a shot in the dark.

What was abundantly clear, however, was that I was doing something wrong.

In hindsight, there were probably a bunch of things wrong. But let's keep it simple. I wasn't talking to the right people. And if one of the right people stumbled across me online, I wasn't saying the right thing to attract them.

Like many frustrated entrepreneurs on a similar path, I tried to figure out how to fix that. I needed to see where my potential clients were lurking online, what they were reading when they needed help, and why they weren't clicking on my name for answers.

Yes, my friends, that led me down the SEO/SEM rabbit hole.

If you're ever feeling masochistic, I highly recommend SEO and SEM. They inflict maximum pain without telltale bruises or scars.

On a more balanced note, there's no shortage of tools or expert consultants who will take your money to get to the top of a search page. But ask them how to do it yourself without constant handholding, or how to turn those searches into sales, and the fog of technobabble descends. Again and again, the exercise left me confused, feeling helpless, and definitely not closer to my target audience.

That said, I believe online search is the best insight and marketing tool out there, for one simple reason.

Search is naked.

When people search, they let their emotional guard down. They expose their true pain points. They aren't in a focus group, giving the moderator answers they think he wants. They aren't rushing through a survey. They aren't cloaking their true intentions or wishes. When they type in "My business needs marketing help," you know that's exactly what they want.

If you can find these anguished cries in the cold, dark Internet night, you've found gold. Provide them with a glimmer of hope, and you'll build instant rapport. Follow up with a real solution, and you'll win a loyal fan. Happy ending.

I believe so strongly in the power of online search (or fish finding, as I like to call it) that I'm actually helping launch a company whose mission is to enable entrepreneurs to crack the code to effective search (https://www.dtermin.com/). My job is designing the experience around the psychology of entrepreneurs. Fast, rewarding, and technobabble-free. Road test it if you like, and let me know what you think.

ASKING FOR IDEAS AND TWEAKS

Yes, it's important to find people online who want to buy your product or service. But if that's all you're asking them to do, you're leaving money on the table.

Let's drop the idea we're online for a moment. If I talked to you in the street, found out we shared the same interests, and discovered you wanted a widget I was selling, that would be the start of a great relationship. Not the conclusion.

Unfortunately, the vast number of companies—both online and offline—drop the ball on this one. They only use their social tools to find clients and make sales. Even if they have the capacity to engage in deeper conversations, they rarely do. You don't often see a company asking consumers for help in creating or tweaking products.

What a waste of brain power.

True, some companies have figured out how to tap consumers for creative input in designing and optimizing products.

For the past few years, Doritos has asked chip lovers to try generically packaged "mystery" flavors and vote for their favorite—the winning flavor lives on in Doritos' permanent lineup (http://adage.com/article/news/doritos-mystery-flavors-test-consumer-loyalty/292713/). It's a good start, but still more of a multiple-choice question rather than a whiteboard session.

Nike+, meanwhile, allows fitness fans to upload their workout information and customize their exercise routines, while giving Nike a treasure trove of information on consumer behavior. This gives Nike great direction for innovating better products. Still, the consumer involvement seems largely unconscious (http://fortune.com/2012/02/13/nikes-new-marketing-mojo/).

Every day, you find stories on consumer data being used to launch new products or tweak existing ones. As I write this, today's story in *Ad Age*—Kraft is modifying its party recipe book to reflect what folks want to serve during Brazil's soccer World Cup. Apparently, Argentine empanadas are trending hot (http://adage.com/article/datadriven-marketing/kraft-makes-data-a-team-player-world-cup-recipe-campaign/294042/?utm_source=cmo_strategy&utm_medium=newsletter&utm_campaign=adage&ttl=1405533845). Again, I wonder if these initiatives are truly about asking consumers how to design better product, or if their involvement is limited to making safe, peripheral decisions?

I don't think we've cracked this one. Perhaps as product design is democratized by the rapidly dropping price of tools like 3-D printers, we'll see more consumers pitching companies their take on products, instead of waiting for those companies to offer them token input. Or highly motivated consumers will take their new designs, build them in the garage, use crowdfunding to launch, and find legions of their own fans. Then they can sell their idea to the big company, or go it alone.

Design thinking embraces this highly creative, messy, human-centric methodology of marketing. As it continues to displace traditional "start with product, just add consumers" thinking, I believe we'll see innovation flourish.

What I do know for certain, though, is that it pays to share ideas with your loyal fans, and get their input. The internet is the world's greatest feedback loop. Let's harness it.

MIND TELLING THE WORLD?

Every day, I get requests from god-knows-who, asking me to like sites filled with god-knows-what.

I hate this.

If you're about to send me a "like" request, be warned: you may push me over the edge. Not only will I not like your site, but I will deface it with virtual graffiti and figure out a way to poke you in the eye with that adorable little thumbs-up icon.

When it comes to getting folks to spread good news, we've once again confused tools with actual social behavior.

In most cases, what we think is social is actually unbelievably antisocial.

Let me illustrate. Imagine someone walks up to you at a party and asks you to like him. Personally, I can't imagine anything creepier. I'd kick him and run away.

Now let's rewind that scenario. Someone walks up to you at a party and tells you the funniest joke ever. What do you do? I'd stick around to hear if she had any more great jokes. Then, when the conversation ended, I'd turn around and tell the next person that mind-bendingly funny joke, pointing out the person who told it to me. Repeat, repeat, repeat.

What most people (and big brands) fail to grasp is that items of little value don't get passed along. When a brand asks you to like it because, well, just because, it usually doesn't happen. And the people that do like it? Probably not influencers who will sway markets with their opinion. Heck, they'd probably like anthrax if you told them to.

Personally, I rarely "like" anything. I'll pass along stories that are smart (and make me look smart by association). I have no qualms about basking in the borrowed glow of your brilliance. It makes me feel as if I've improved the world in some small way.

But not all brands have a great story to share. Or do they?

I'm a firm believer virtually every brand was founded for a good reason. Nobody wakes up and decides to invent something new just because. It's simply too much work, and solutions without problems don't last.

Assuming this is true, we simply have to discover that reason, understand how the founder translated it into a new product or service, and find out how it changed peoples' lives. If we want more material, we can dig into some of the highlights of the brand's evolution. There are stories in there somewhere, probably loaded with anecdotes of perserverance, setbacks and breakthroughs.

Want proof? Go online and check out the story of any established brand. You'll find fodder for great storytelling buried beneath the mountains of milque toast, minimum risk marketing that make the brand a commodity today. Some examples I unearthed with minimal searching:

- Tampax – The ancient Egyptians, Greeks and Roman all 'invented' tampons. In World War II, Tampax were used to dress wounds (http://www.tampax.com/en-us/about-tampax.aspx). Their inventor, meanwhile, was named one of the Thousand Makers of the 20th Century by the London Sunday Times (https://www.periodbox.co.uk/blog/history-of-tampons/).

- Interflora – Started in 1910, the company created its famous 'Mercury Man' logo in 1914. Following World War II, florists were flown from the US to the UK to train new recruits, as many older florists had lost their lives in the war. And in 1991, astronaut Helen Sharman sent the first Interflora order from space (http://www.interflora.co.uk/content/becoming-flower-experts/).

- John Deere – The Furrow, John Deere's newsletter first published in 1895, became the world's preeminent farmer's magazine. The Model D tractor remained in the product line for 30 years. There was a "John Deere Battalion" in World War II (https://www.deere.com/en_US/corporate/our_company/about_us/history/timeline/timeline.page).

You get the point.

Word of mouth is probably the most potent media out there. My advice to anyone trying to effectively tap this incredible resource is to create something worth talking about. Human stories, stories worth passing on. This means turning off the computer and firing up your imagination.

CONCLUSION

So, how do we wrap a ribbon around this story, and make it something you can tell your friend about in a thirty second elevator ride?

You might be able to say you discovered some useful tools for building brands in chaotic times. I kinda doubt it. There are stacks of books out there that can provide lists, charts, case studies and step-by-steps guaranteed to improve your game. But be cautioned – I've spent my life reading airport business advice books. The only people who tend to benefit from them are the authors.

Maybe this book will give you a bead on nascent trends and how to respond to them. Probably not, though. Research and experience can tell us what consumers want today. Only intuition and a willingness to abandon our preconceptions and beliefs will enable us to see what consumers might want in the future.

At the end of the day, I believe this book will have fulfilled its purpose if it leaves you scratching your head, wondering what surprises the world has in store and how you're going to react.

Truly, there is no better way to go through life.

I have met too many people who were certain about the future, or their marketing expertise, or how person A will respond if you apply stimulus B. These people were drinking their own bathwater. Or perhaps they were just trying to suppress that voice bubbling up inside them. You know, the one that says "Oh really?" in a snarky tone.

In my daily life, I help clients build brands that are resilient enough to withstand the shocks of an unstable world. Those brands all seem to have three fundamental qualities:

- They know themselves.
- They trust the intangible, human bond with their audience.
- They listen. Really listen.

It seems ridiculous that I could spend twenty-five years in this field, and come away with just three simple pieces of knowledge to share. A bit unsettling, the feeling your contribution to humanity can be written on a cocktail napkin.

Then again, there were only ten commandments. And most folks (meaning me) can only remember the kill, steal, and oxen-coveting ones.

Good luck. And, please, if you have wisdom to share that would enhance my theories on building better brands for the future, get in touch.

I'm eager to learn.

ABOUT THE AUTHOR

MARC STOIBER

Marc Stoiber is a creative strategist, entrepreneur, and writer.

At previous points in his life, he's been VP Green Innovation at Maddock Douglas, Founder of Change Advertising, National Creative Director of Grey Canada, Creative Director of DDB Toronto, and Copywriter at BBDO Dusseldorf and Grey Hong Kong. His first writing job was translating a kung fu movie. Really.

He writes on brand innovation for Huffington Post, Fast Company, GreenBiz and Sustainable Life Media. He also speaks on the subject from coast to coast, and has been featured at TEDx. He can be reached at:

marc@marcstoiber.com

Made in the USA
Charleston, SC
09 May 2015